TRUTH
APPLIED

Books in the Jay Adams Library

TRUTH APPLIED

Application in Preaching

Jay E. Adams

Ministry Resources Library

Zondervan Publishing House • Grand Rapids, MI

TRUTH APPLIED
Copyright © 1990 by Jay E. Adams

Ministry Resources Library is an imprint of Zondervan Publishing House,
1415 Lake Drive, S.E., Grand Rapids, Michigan 49506.

Library of Congress Cataloging in Publication Data

Adams, Jay Edward.
    Truth applied : application in preaching / Jay E. Adams.
        p.   cm.
    ISBN 0-310-51031-7
    1. Preaching. I. Title.
BV4211.2.A335   1990   89-78072
251—dc20   CIP

Unless otherwise indicated, all New Testament quotations are from the
Christian Counselor's New Testament.

Edited by Gerard Terpstra
Designed by Louise Bauer

Printed in the United States of America

90 91 92 93 94 95 / CH / 10 9 8 7 6 5 4 3 2 1

To
My Doctor of Ministry Students
Fellow Conspirators
in the
Grand Enterprise

Contents

Preface

When Haddon Robinson wrote,

> Many homileticians have not given application the attention it deserves. No book has been published devoted exclusively, or even primarily to the knotty problems raised by application.[1]

he was expressing the felt need that brought forth this volume. Doubtless other homileticians and preachers concur in recognizing the lack that Robinson is aware of. Many a man, having been given little or no warning that the way of application runs through rough terrain, has stubbed his toe on the rock of application. Others, knowing all too well the pitfalls—perhaps from having plummeted headlong into some themselves—have retreated, fearing to pass that way again, and are thus depriving their congregations of the blessings of the living Word of God addressed to the modern scene. It is my purpose, therefore, to attempt to fill this void as adequately as I can by considering a number of those knotty problems of which Robinson speaks and untying as many as I can.

"But," you may ask, "why is there such a lack? What has kept the homiliticians from dealing with application in

[1]Haddon Robinson, *Biblical Preaching* (Grand Rapids: Baker, 1980), 89.

depth?" Various answers suggest themselves: (1) Little has been written about preaching in general, much less about specific aspects of preaching; (2) relying on the faulty scholastic methods that many seminaries have taught regarding applying the Scriptures, most preachers are unaware of the knotty problems involved; (3) to present biblically derived principles of application means that someone must do the hard work of distilling such principles from the Scriptures. Up to now this has not been done; (4) to adopt biblical principles of application undoubtedly would radically alter, and might severely limit, present undisciplined preaching practices.

These reasons might be thought formidable enough to deter anyone from tackling the task of searching out biblical principles of application. But I have not been known for taking on easy tasks in practical theology, and I certainly don't intend to let a few difficult problems stand in the way. I trust that after you have read this book you will agree that, if nothing more, you have been challenged to reconsider your present theory and practice of application. If so, I will have helped you. But I think you will receive far more. In this volume I believe I have truly untied some of the knots Robinson had in mind. You must be the one to judge whether I have been successful.

This book does not address the reasons for the homileticians' lack of concern about application, but rather, it presents what I hope you will agree is a cogent, biblical philosophy of application, together with practical suggestions about how the busy preacher can readily implement it. Read and see.

Introduction

What you read in the pages to follow may run counter to many of your present practices. I want to warn you at the outset that it could radically change your preaching ministry. If you are not looking for a challenge, for something fresh, something that will make a difference in the future, stop reading now. Indeed, if this book fails to stir your interest (and perhaps at times even your ire), if it doesn't correct and change some of your ways of preparing and delivering sermons, then writing it has been a futile exercise.

Obviously, my purpose is to change your understanding and use of application in preaching (insofar as that is necessary). I ask you to compare and contrast what you have been taught in the past with the views and methods that this book advocates. Why? Because, in my opinion, application has been largely misunderstood and, consequently, mistaught. I urge you to think carefully about what I say to see if I am right.

Let's take an example. Have you ever had the uneasy feeling that when you reach the place in your sermon where you customarily apply the exposition or the doctrine you have been teaching, that you are beginning to tread the same ground again? Doesn't the repetition of what you are saying—this running around in circles that application seems to require, even though you are now talking about the contemporary scene—bother you?

Or consider this: you have spent thirty minutes on exposition and now you find you must hurry the application along at the end, cutting it short because you have run out of time. Does that ever happen? "No," you say, "because I always apply my teaching at the conclusion of each point; so I don't have to wait to the end." What about the last point? Do you ever slight application of it for lack of time? And—think this through—if you apply each point before moving to the next, do your sermons seem to run all over the map, without any unifying purpose? Or, to keep them from doing that, do you have to pull all the applications together, repeating them in the conclusion, to show how they congeal into the one main application that was your purpose for preaching the sermon?

Some preachers simply make the application the final point of the sermon. But because that is just another way of tacking on application at the end, it doesn't solve the problems mentioned above. As a matter of fact, it creates new, additional problems, especially when alloting the application the space of a full point in the message means curtailing exposition or teaching in order to "fit application in."

Do you ever have an uneasy conscience over the way you applied a text? How can you be sure you are not misapplying the truth of God's Word? Do you wonder what constitutes legitimate application of a passage to the contemporary scene? Have you asked yourself whether a passage may have more than one application and, if so, how many?

And how about your congregation? Do the people have difficulty bringing the Bible up to date in their own lives? Do they seem to view it as a Book having to do principally with the hoary past? Do the boys in the back row wonder what "all this stuff about Paul and the Corinthians" has to do with them? Does your sermon seem to you and the congregation like a direct word from God to them about their lives? Do they listen to you as a congregation being addressed by God through His messenger just as surely as if the preaching portion (the Scripture portion you are using as the source of your message) were originally written to them? Do you preach that way? In other words, does your preaching convey the fact that the Bible is a living Book that applies to them just as truly as it did to the Corinthians?

If you are having problems with any or all of these matters that grow out of inadequate applicatory practices, then read carefully what follows. In the chapters to come I intend to show you how to overcome not only each of the problems mentioned but also a number of others. And in the process I intend to point you to a way of applying the Scriptures that not only is true to their purpose but that, when properly understood and implemented, will also make all the difference to you and your congregation. Are you ready? Then let's begin.

1

What Is Application?

When you "apply" pressure to a wound, you make forceful contact with it in order to stop the bleeding. When you give a dingy wall a fresh "application" of paint, you lay paint onto the wall in such a way that it sticks and thereby affects the looks of the wall. When you speak of "applied" science, you mean theory worked out in various useful ways that make a difference in everyday living. To "apply" is to bring one thing into contact with another in such a way that the two adhere, so that what is applied *to* something affects that to which it is applied. The pressure stops the bleeding, the paint freshens the wall, and the theory changes daily life in practical ways.

The idea of applying flows from two Latin words that, through the French, are combined into one word. The words are *ap (ad)*="to" and *plico*="to knit." Thus they came to mean to "knit" or "join" something (or oneself) "to" something else. In time, this developed into the thought of knitting or joining *in such a way as to change or effect that to which something is joined.*

In homiletics, the term *application* has come to be

applied to one aspect of preaching (in this sentence I am using the verb *apply* to mean much the same thing as I did when speaking of "applying" paint to a wall: the word *application*, I am saying, has become *attached to* a process that occurs in faithful preaching).

For a long time other terms vied with *application* before it gained the ascendency. Two, in particular, stand out: *improvement* and *use*.

To "improve" the text (as preachers used to say) did not mean to tamper with the biblical passage to make it better. Rather, the idea was for the preacher to so use the text in his preaching as to make it profitable, or useful, to the listener. To "improve," then, meant to exploit, cash in on, take advantage of, or turn something to account. Improved land is land that has been made more useful by cultivation, the addition of utilities, etc. So, actually, "improving" the text meant improving the congregation by enabling them to utilize God's truth in daily living.

The other term, *use*, meant much the same thing. The effective preacher told his congregation how the truth of his preaching portion could be put to use. Puritan preachers often divided their sermons into two large sections (sometimes more):

1. The *Doctrines* (or teachings) that they "gathered" (culled and abstracted) from the passage, and

2. The *Uses* that these teachings might have in everyday living. Sometimes the uses in a sermon were numbered in the twenties (or higher!).

In the end, the word *application* won out over the other terms. Why this is so is not altogether clear. It is my conjecture that the reason is to be found in the more active, aggressive denotation that the word came to have. As we noted in the discussion of the word above—whether it is used in reference to applying pressure on a wound, applying paint to a wall, or applying scientific theory to life—there is always the idea that something is affected by the act of applying. Paint properly applied to a wall colors it, a label applied to a process identifies it, pressure applied to a wound actually stops bleeding, and theory applied to life changes living.

I suspect that the word *application* won out, therefore, because it spoke of actually accomplishing something through preaching rather than merely informing others about the possibility of doing so. To *improve* the text is to make it useful to the listener—*if* he or she cares to take advantage of it. To explain the *uses* to which a passage may be put, again, does not mean that one induces the listener to actually so use it. To *apply*, however, seems to connote (if it does not actually denote) that a preacher so brings the purpose of his preaching portion to bear on the members of a congregation that they are in some way *more than informed* (if they are not moved to action, at least they are made to squirm!). Applying the truth of a passage, then, also involves exerting pressure on the congregation to implement it. Be that as it may, the word *application* did emerge the victor and, like it or not, we are stuck with it.

So, to sum up, *application* is the word currently used to denote that process by which preachers make scriptural truths so pertinent to members of their congregations that they not only understand how those truths should effect changes in their lives but also feel obligated and perhaps even eager to implement those changes.

2

Is Application Necessary?

Some think that application is not a necessary part of a sermon. Others seem to equate application with meaning. Still others think application is impossible. In the mind of the preacher who is conversant with the various views concerning application, the question must seem vexing indeed.

Even though the use of application is currently in jeopardy, it has a long history in the church. Of course, longevity can never be the determining factor for the biblical preacher: some tradition may well be erroneous and harmful. Because of this fact and because of assaults made on application (both by direct attack and by insidious neglect), it is important to spend some time justifying the use of application in preaching.

In *Prayer and Preaching* Karl Barth writes uncertainly about application. He maintains that a preacher need not call the congregation "to make decisions." If any decisions are made, it is through a "direct encounter between man and God"—an encounter in which the preacher plays no part: "the decision does not depend on him."[1] Barth says, "A

---

[1]Karl Barth, *Prayer and Preaching* (London: SCM, 1964), 66.

serious difficulty presents itself in regard to application: how to be faithful to the text and also true to life." To this difficulty, he claims, "there is *no solution.*"[2] Clearly, Barth thinks it is impossible for human beings to apply Scripture; this task belongs to God alone. The preacher must speak about the text and about life today, but God must bridge the gap, applying as He pleases what He will. Application, as far as the preacher is concerned, should at most be inferential, not direct. Direct application might prejudice the decision-encounter.

Elements of this neoorthodox approach seem to have influenced conservatives, especially many of those who claim to do "biblical-theological preaching."

I am not impuning the use of biblical theology. Indeed, biblical theology helps the preacher avoid moralizing and makes a sermon Christian. But a preacher should no more be known as a "biblical-theological *preacher*" than he should be known as a "systematic-theological *preacher.*" As a preacher of the Word, he is ideally both a theologian and an exegete, using both theology and exegesis in the preparation of his messages. Properly used in sermon preparation, both systematic and biblical theology play important, indeed, essential roles. But when the minister of the Word reduces a sermon to little more than a biblical-theological lecture (or meditation), he is no more preaching than if he were delivering a lecture on systematic theology.[3]

Conservative biblical-theological preachers, sailing in the wake of Gerhardus Vos,[4] tend to ignore (or even

---

[2]Ibid., 108 (emphasis mine).

[3]For a longer discussion of this point, see Jay Adams, "The Proper Use of Biblical Theology in Preaching," *The Journal of Pastoral Practice* 9, no. 1: 47–49.

[4]For a good example of the sort of biblical-theological sermon about which I am speaking, see Gerhardus Vos, *Grace and Glory* (Grand Rapids: Reformed Press, 1922). Although these sermons are beautifully written and full of instructive matter, there is no application in them. Sometimes young pastors are intimidated by the charge that application is "moralistic." But morality is not the same as moralism: the former is biblical and Christ-honoring; the latter is not.

oppose) the use of application in a sermon. They expect the listener to make his own application (if any) of the sweeping truths they set forth on their excursions from Genesis to Revelation as they chase down a figure or a theme. Or, like Barth, they leave the application to God. The two major differences between some present-day preachers and Barth is that the former (1) do not hold to the neoorthodox "encounter," and (2) are less concerned about the contemporary scene than Barth.

Abhorrence of direct application leads biblical-theological preachers of this sort into common ground with many liberals who believe that the use of the indicative alone, to the exclusion of the imperative, is adequate. At best, such preaching is applied (if at all) by implication; at worst, only by inference. Application becomes the task of the listener rather than the preacher.

POSITION AND APPLICATION

When you preach, what is your position in regard to both the Scripture text and your congregation? Or, putting it another way, with whom do you, *as a preacher*, identify? There are at least three options. Whichever one of these you choose will make all the difference in how successfully you apply the truth. Let's take a hard look at each of these three options: spectator, recipient, and herald.

Position 1: Spectator

If you adopt the first possible position in the pulpit, you will identify with no one in your sermon material or in the congregation. Indeed, you will make a concerted effort not to do so. The speaker or the crowd mentioned in the text, or the recipient(s) of an epistle, will be seen as "out there." The congregation also will be viewed as onlookers. You will position yourself *outside* the text and at a convenient distance from the congregation. You will be like a bystander, a spectator rather than a participant.

Perhaps the analogy of a cameraman will make this point clearer. The cameraman, while not participating in the event itself, because he stands behind the camera rather than before it, *enables* the TV viewer to see and hear what is happening on the set.

The task of the preacher-as-cameraman is to zoom in on the passage in order to capture and portray the action as fully and advantageously as possible.

The type of preaching one does when he positions himself in this mode usually is the sort of biblical-theological preaching I have been describing. Taking large sweeps across the biblical landscape, often traveling through centuries (and even millennia) with ease, these cameramen-preachers seldom use "tight" shots in which closeups of the text are provided. They prefer the big picture rather than details. Their preaching is often impressionistic, lacking in fine detail, and it frequently leaves the listener with only a vague or hazy idea of the purpose of any given passage.

Also comfortable with this mode are preachers at the opposite extreme, for to them, minute detail is precisely the concern. In these constant closeups—often labeled expository or inductive preaching—*telos* (end, or purpose) is lost because of concentration on trivia.

In this attitudinal mode may be found the expository magician who performs before his dazzled congregation amazing feats of exegetical legerdemain. "Watch closely now," you can virtually hear him say, "as I pull rabbits out of this verse that you would never have believed were there." Using first this trick and then that from his bag of expository tricks, he wows his congregation with new "insights" from week to week. The people come to church equipped with pen, notebook, and reference Bibles, fully prepared to record for posterity every fresh insight wafted on the wings of his word.[5]

While the biblical-theological preacher ordinarily ex-

---

[5]The problem is not new. In his sermons on Titus, Calvin says, "They seem to be great teachers because they treat of somewhat subtle and nice points." (John Calvin, *Sermons on the Epistles to Timothy and Titus* (Edinburgh: Banner of Truth Trust, reprint 1983), 1140). I have modernized the language slightly.

pects the members of his congregation to make their own applications, with little help from him, some gospel magicians may make brief applications all along the way (often so many that no one application predominates). But these applications are like fruit that appears out on the end of the branches of the tree, each piece having little relationship to the rest. There is no unity to the sermon. The magician's focus is not on application, nor is it on purpose. Instead, he emphasizes knowledge—usually of an esoteric (at times almost gnostic) sort. He will talk much of "edification by the truth," sometimes claiming to be a "Bible teacher" rather than a "preacher," but most frequently he will insist that he is an "expository preacher."

Despite the obvious differences between the two sorts of preachers that I have characterized as assuming the spectator position in the pulpit, they hold important elements in common:

1. Neither sees preaching *as application*. If and when he applies the impressions he creates or the knowledge he imparts, the application is quite secondary to the exposition.

2. In the preaching of both types of preachers, the third person dominates the sermon. Sermons tend to be abstract, in the past tense, and freckled with "he, she, they, it, and them." Truth is "set forth," hung out there on the line to flap in the breeze, but it is rarely driven home to effect change.

3. All preachers who preach from behind the camera refuse to identify with the writer of the passage, the recipient(s) of the book, or anyone mentioned in the text. Their doting congregations view them as "masters" of the text, men with a massive grasp of the Bible, who hover above it in some ethereal realm.

4. Both sorts of preachers believe that their preaching method is the only legitimate one. If the history of redemption is not *the focus of the sermon*, the biblical-theological preacher considers it inadequate, at best a specious form of moralism. If a preacher fails to minutely dissect the preaching

portion, uncovering various and sundry oddities not usually observed by others, the expository magician who hears him derides the sermon as "trivial and trite"—at best, superficial, "lacking meat."

Position 2: Recipient

Those preachers who adopt the position of recipient are (generally) more concerned about application than those who opt for the position of spectator. They are also a less easily defined group than those who adopt either of the other positions. Perhaps one could say that their preaching, considered from the perspective of application, forms the great hump in the bell curve of preaching, with preaching in positions 1 and 3 sliding down to the bottom of the curve on either side. What sets off the preaching of those in position 2 from the others is not their lack of zeal for any one method or emphasis in preaching, but their deep concern not to be thought dogmatic, holier-than-thou, or arrogant.

This concern causes them to identify with the recipient(s) of the biblical book, both the people to whom Jesus, Paul, or some other person was speaking in the text and the congregations to which they are now delivering their sermons. Not only will you hear them regularly using the first person plural ("we"), but there may also be a fair amount of reference to themselves in the first person singular ("I"). These preachers are *self*-conscious. They want to come across to congregations as being one of them. You will often hear them saying such things as "I am no different from you," "What I am saying applies equally to me," and "Whenever I point a finger at you, I realize there are three pointing at me." Thus, by their extreme reticence, they dull whatever application they may make.

You will notice that many of these preachers quickly picked up a current cliché: "Now, let me *share* something with you." The word *share* used in this way is weak. When a preacher "shares," he does not declare or proclaim. He is not on the spot. He does not have to prove he is God's messenger or has God's message. How can you hold someone accountable for what he says when he is only "sharing"?

Biblical preachers are not called to share the gospel; they must preach the *whole* of the Good News. The idea of "sharing" indicates that what the preacher is saying is incomplete, only a portion of a truth, his portion of a larger group experience. As he is "just one of" the congregation, so too his experience is but a part of the experience of the whole. Clearly, the notion of "sharing" places the preacher in the pulpit and the congregation gathered before him on the same footing.

What position-2 preachers fear, in particular, is the use of "you" in preaching: "People would think me arrogant should I preach in the second person." Even while appreciating their concern not to "lord it over the flock," one must nevertheless point out the fallacy of their thinking. It is not arrogant for God's appointed servant to proclaim God's Word directly, even pointedly, to those to whom He addresses it.

Indeed, if the ordained minister of the Word is no different from those to whom he preaches, it is the epitome of arrogance for him to preach at all. Why is he standing there before the congregation? If he is only "one of them," then he ought to take his place out there among them. If his role is no different from theirs, then, when he preaches, he is arrogance personified. He must have a special appointment and authority to preach; that unique role alone qualifies him to preach. If position 2 is the correct one, there is no reason for the congregation to "honor" him for "his work's sake" (1 Thess. 5:13). The recipient position ("God is speaking to all of us this morning, including me")[6] *confuses*

---

[6]Notice how position 2 requires the preacher to keep referring to himself (even in using the word *we*, he does so). This, in time, is likely to become a subtle form of arrogance, or at least, of undue self-importance. When he ought to be calling attention to God as the One who has a message for His congregation, instead, he unwittingly communicates that the message is his. "Sharing," mentioned earlier, also shifts the emphasis from God's objective message to the preacher's subjective experience, thus putting man in the place of God.

the preacher's personal life as a Christian with his role as one set apart to declare God's Word.

Luther said,

> You must distinctly separate the two, the office and the person. . . . When he administers his office . . . a man is different . . . a man is not a preacher by virtue of personal authority but by authority vested in him by God.[7]

That is the biblical position, articulated in the Reformation and held by all evangelical churches ever since.

Surely every preacher, in one sense, must be as fully involved in the text as his congregation is. He too must be a recipient—but long before, in his study. He must also ask the Spirit of God to enable him to be a "spectator" in the sense that he wants truly to observe everything in the preaching portion *apart from* any unbiblical bias that might otherwise cloud his understanding. And, having correctly understood it, he will want to become a personal recipient of truth, applying the passage to his own life. But positions 1 and 2 belong to the study and the home. The preacher, as a Bible student, must become a keen observer of Scripture, missing neither important details in the preaching portion nor the relationship of these details to the bigger picture in the history of redemption.

So the person is to be a scholar in the study but a preacher in the pulpit. As an individual and a needy sinner, he too is a recipient of God's message—it should powerfully affect him before he enters the pulpit. But he has not been called to "share." Once he stands before God's flock to feed His sheep as an overseeing shepherd (1 Peter 5:2), he may not assume positions in reference to the preaching portion of his sermon or his congregation that have to do with his personal life (other than illustratively, of course). He must relegate personal concerns to the study and to society. This fact, then, leads us to a discussion of the third position.

---

[7]Ewald M. Plais, ed., *What Luther Says*, 3 vols. (St. Louis: Concordia, 1959), 3:1113.

Position 3: Herald

A minister stands before God's people neither as an objective observer (position 1) nor in his own right (position 2), but as a "man from God" (2 Tim. 3:17). He is a *keryx* (the Greek word for "herald"). He is one who is sent from God (Rom. 10:15), bearing God's Word, an appointed agent through whom God addresses people. The herald is a person with authority, one commissioned to deliver messages from God. In the *pulpit*, therefore, he identifies, not with the recipients of God's Word, but with God; he also identifies with the writers of biblical books and with Jesus and the apostles whenever they speak in various preaching portions. Identify with the right person and you will know how you ought to preach. Then, and only then, will you be in a proper relationship to God and your congregation. As Calvin put it, "He who goes into the pulpit to preach, is there in the authority and name of the Son of God."[8]

The dominant pronoun in his preaching is *you*. The first-person pronoun rarely occurs; the third-person pronoun occurs only in opening the Scriptures to show what God did or said in the past *as the basis for what He is doing or saying now*. The prevailing tenses he uses are the present and the future. The herald preaches the Bible, not as a book describing what God did or said in time past, but as God's present Word to the people of God gathered before him. Having studied with a contemporary perspective, the herald comes to God's flock with a message fresh from God. His whole sermon, therefore, is application.

"Well, I can understand that much of what you say is true, but how does a preacher avoid such charges as those of arrogance and an attitude of self-importance that the position-two recipient dreads?"

Of course, it is possible for the herald to abuse his authority by arrogating it to himself as though it were not conferred on him by God. If he does so, he actually moves out of the position of a herald. Diotrophes did this when he confused his *personal* status with his status *as a herald*. The

---

[8]Calvin, *Timothy and Titus*, 950.

herald's authority is always a conferred authority (*exousia*), not personally generated authority (*dynamis*). Authority is not authoritarianism. For the authoritarian preacher, the weight of the proclamation depends on him as the herald; for the preacher who has authority, the weight of the proclamation depends on the One who sent him.

In the pulpit the herald represents God, not himself. He is not his own person. He will always be tempted to abuse rather than use his authority, and he must carefully guard against doing so. But in spite of the temptation, he may not shirk his responsibility to use authority properly. In speaking of this problem of authority, Paul once wrote of the "authority that the Lord gave us for building ... up and not for tearing ... down" (2 Cor. 10:8). But precisely because he understood the divine purpose of authority, he did not hesitate to deal sharply with congregations when necessary (cf. 2 Cor. 13:10).

"But I thought the word *minister* means 'servant.' How, then can he exercise authority?"

The hotel manager is a servant. His job is to serve the guests. He must see that they are comfortable, make sure their rooms are clean, and assure them of swift and pleasant service. But if guests would begin to cart TVs from their rooms, roll up the rugs to take them home, and remove pictures from the wall, he would not offer them his help with a smile! He would forbid them to continue their pillage, and if they would not listen, he would call the police. What would have caused this servant to change?

The answer is that the manager, first and foremost, is the servant of the owner. Ordinarily, he serves him by serving his guests. But when the guests get out of line, his service to the owner supersedes service to the guests. He exercises the authority that his owner invested in him by removing them from the premises. Of course, in many ways, he also exercises authority for the convenience and pleasure of acceptable guests.

Similarly, the preacher serves God by serving His people. But, like the manager, he has authority in that service and uses it as needed. In declaring and enforcing the Owner's rules, he serves God, and actually—whether his service is so recognized or not—he serves the church as well. Service and authority are complementary, not contradictory.

Part of the problem is that people living in a democracy that stresses pluralism and individualism and sometimes borders on anarchy find it difficult to submit to authority. If they don't like what is going on in one church, they simply move to another. They recognize no authority. The preacher must be sure he does not contribute to this weakening of church authority by assuming some position lower than that of the herald. Indeed, in times like these, it is all the more essential for the preacher to instruct congregations about his authority, as Paul did. Moreover, when the preacher exercises authority in accordance with the Scriptures, not "lording it over God's flock" but using it to "build up" the flock, he reestablishes respect for Christ's authority in the church.

"But how can he avoid charges of 'lording it over the flock'?"

Let me answer that question in two ways. First, of course, he must be sure that he is not in fact doing so. It is easy to deceive oneself. Alertness and self-examination (especially of motives), along with prayerful solicitation of the Holy Spirit's help, are the basic prerequisites for avoiding self-deceit. Then if one is truly humble when acting as a herald, his servant attitude will be obvious to others.

There are, however, persons who resist all authority, refusing to recognize the humility of anyone who exercises authority. The preacher cannot avoid charges from such persons, though the charges may be totally unfounded. Even the apostle of love was subjected to the abuses of a rebellious preacher who refused to recognize his authority (3 John 9–10). A faithful preacher may expect abuses and accusations. To counter the rebellious attitudes of others, precisely what the preacher needs is authority.

But, second, let me suggest one or two ways that you may be able to blunt the edge of any charge of arrogance while, at the same time, properly exerting your God-given authority as herald. One good way to suggest *indirectly* that you do not "think more highly of yourself than you ought to think" (Rom. 12:3), is to use examples and illustrations from your own life in which you "goofed," failed, or were the butt of some joke. If you can show in your sermons that you also struggle with problems or that you often need gentle reminders from a caring wife, for example, members of your congregation who do not resist authority will recognize clearly how you make a distinction between you as a person and you as a preacher.

It is always possible to overdo the use of personal examples. You can also by certain illustrations put yourself in such a bad light that people will lose confidence in you. For the most part, it is wise to confine personal illustrations to your lighter foibles. The pulpit is not a confessional. The purpose of illustrations is to illustrate, not to talk about yourself. Your emphasis must always be on God and the congregation, never on yourself. While you must make your presence felt, it must always be as one who speaks for God.

There may, of course, be times when what you have to say is so wonderful that it is hard for people to believe it. Or your message may involve a rebuke that is hard to take. On such occasions it may be wise to emphasize *directly* your position as a herald: "Don't think I have invented this stupendous truth out of whole cloth. This is *God's* gracious promise!" Or, in regard to a rebuke: "Please listen carefully to what God says. *He's* the One who says this, not I!"

Because so many in the modern church resist authority, preachers retreat to the first or second position, becoming spectators or fellow recipients. This retreat has only exacerbated the problem. We will never restore biblical care and discipline to Christ's church until we establish respect for preaching. This will come only when preachers take up their rightful position as heralds of the Lord Jesus Christ.

You are driving down the street and run a red light. A police car comes out of nowhere and tails you with light flashing. You pull over. The officer gets out of his car, comes to your window, and says, "We went through a red light, didn't we? Let's have a look at our licenses. I will write us a ticket, and we will have to pay a fine or go to jail."

"Ridiculous!" you say.

Of course. But no more ridiculous than some preachers sound. The policeman comes with authority. He says, "You went through a red light. Let me see your license, etc." He uses the second person "you" throughout the unpleasant experience. And, though you are not at all happy about the incident, you do not call him "arrogant" because he exercised his rightful authority and by a proper use of vocabulary demonstrated clearly toward whom it was directed. Now, tell me, why should you accept the authority of God vested in the state and in the police officer as its agent and not accept the authority of God's Word vested in His church and in its agent, the preacher?

But forget all I have said for the moment, if you will, and discover for yourself what New Testament preaching was like. With a highlighter pen in hand, read the recorded sermons of John the Baptist, Jesus, Peter, and Paul, highlighting every second-person pronoun used. At the conclusion of this exercise you will have the most colorful Bible in town! And—you will have effectively demonstrated to yourself that biblical preaching is authoritative.

In summary, consider the following chart:

Three Positions

Spectator	Recipient	Herald
Identifies with no one in the text, nor with the congregation	Identifies with recipient of message and with congregation	Identifies with God and writer/speaker in the text
Abstract, past tense, third person (he, she, it, they, them)	First person (we, our, I)	Concrete, present tense, second person (you)
"The Amalekites . . . they"	"I'm just one of you"	"God says you . . ."
	"We are told in this passage . . ."	

Is application necessary? Absolutely. And the reason is that preaching is heralding. It is not mere exposition. It is not lecturing on history—even redemptive history. It is not "sharing." It is authoritatively declaring both the good and the bad news of the Bible. It is forcefully bringing home to God's people God's message from God's Word.

3

Truth Applied

. . . the Prophets were preachers, and . . . there are two kinds of preaching. There is what we may call "Academic" preaching, the unfolding of ideas and truths for the sake of the ideas and truths themselves. A man may take a principle and unfold it, and explain it, illustrate it and adorn it, for the sheer joy of doing this. It is always an interesting work to take an idea or principle and give an exposition of it, unfolding its beauty, exploring its meaning. Many men rejoice in that sort of intellectual work, and many other people greatly enjoy seeing them do it. A preacher who preaches in this way does not apply his principle or his truth to the problems of society. He is not especially interested in conduct. . . .

On the other hand, there is "Practical" preaching. When a man preaches practically, he always applies his ideas to the . . . problems of the day. He is interested supremely in life, and the object of his preaching is to bring his ideas to bear upon life. . . . The prophets were practical preachers. They never preached academically. . . . They were easily understood by the persons who heard them.

I am, as you know, a practical preacher. I never preach academically. I am not interested in abstractions in the pulpit. In my library at home, with books of philosophy around me, I can have a good time in the realm of theory and speculation, but as soon as I get into the pulpit, I am always practical; that is, I am always dealing with life as I see it around me. I care nothing for the unfolding of ideas unless I can apply them to the conduct of individuals and institutions. I am always preaching to the twentieth century. No other century has any controlling interest for me.[1]

Jefferson has pinpointed the problem and the general solution to it, but he neglects the particulars. *how* does one preach practically rather than academically? (In my terminology, how does one *preach* instead of *lecture?*) How does one take universal truth, clothed in ancient garb and directed as it was toward outmoded situations, and redirect it to life in the computer age? That is what we must begin to explore in this chapter and those that follow.

THE BIBLICAL FORM

Secretly some people—even preachers—express their dislike for the Bible. They wonder:

Why did God write the Bible the way He did? Why didn't he make it easier to use? The Bible really isn't "user friendly." For instance, if He had set it up in encyclopedic form, whenever I needed to know anything about adultery, I'd simply turn to the A volume, where I could read a comprehensive article on it. If I needed information about child rearing, volume C, and so on.

---

[1]Charles Jefferson, *Cardinal Ideas of Isaiah* (New York: Macmillan, 1931), 23–26. In the same book he also said, "The Old Testament prophets were ethical teachers, not teaching ethics alone, but always insisting that religion shall issue in conduct" (87). Further on in the book he says, "It is not until ideas are translated into American thought that they have any influence over us" (170).

Doubtless, there are advantages to an encyclopedia. It is a handy, easy-to-use reference. But the purpose of an encyclopedia is to provide information, whereas the purpose of the Bible is to change life. The form of each is adapted to its own purpose. The Spirit knew what He was doing when He moved men to write the Bible out of their life experiences.

The form in which the Bible has come to us *forces* us to study it in ways in which we would never think of studying an encyclopedia. For instance, we must know all about the grammar, the history, and the rhetorical, literary, systematic, and biblical-theological background of a passage and why it was written if we are to understand its message. We must learn the relationship of the people involved in any given passage to God and their neighbors. We must see God in action. We must understand how the redemption of Christ relates to every sort of activity of every sort of person that there is. You don't concern yourself with such matters when turning to an entry in an encyclopedia.

In the Bible we face facts, but far more than facts: on the pages of Scripture we face God Himself! We see Him in action, hear Him address us in our sins and need, and, as we read, listen to His call, not merely to learn, but to repent, believe, and love—as well as think. The Bible is a Book that encourages God's child to love Him and to love his neighbor by trusting the gospel and following Jesus Christ. That—not mere information—is its purpose In short, in the Bible you find *truth applied.*

Doubtless, pastor, your task would be lightened, in some ways, if the Bible were in encyclopedic form, but neither your life nor that of your congregation would be largely affected by what you read. That would give rise to a new and greater problem. You would forfeit examples of truth in action, God in reaction to man's failures, consequences of failures, and sins. That too would be a great loss.

Of course, it would be possible to write all about this in an "academic" fashion in the encyclopedia. But how would that replace the parables, the Old Testament narratives, the heartbeat of the Psalms? An encyclopedic account of the Crucifixion and the Resurrection would hardly move you to faith and gratitude. But, described in terms of the interaction of the Savior, God, the disciples, and the enemies of Christ, all the understanding, pathos, and richness of the event comes through. The Bible's accounts of life are multidimensional in a way no encyclopedia could ever be. An encyclopedia record of the work of missions would hardly inspire you to volunteer to become a missionary! An encyclopedia description of love could never produce it.

The encyclopedia has its place—as an aid to gathering incidental information for preaching—but it could never be the *basis* for preaching. Since God designed the Bible as, among other things, a preaching text, in it He provided a variety of literary forms and approaches. In it you encounter the whole gamut of human experience, and in it He revealed His truth in an applied form.

If this is so, what does it tell us about preaching?

TELIC PREACHING

First, I will repeat briefly what I have dwelt on at great length in an earlier book, *Preaching With Purpose*.[2] In that book my concern was to show that much preaching has failed because God's *telos* (or purpose) in the preaching passage has been ignored by preachers who, instead, use it for their own purposes, thereby misusing it and losing the force of the passage.

Perhaps I can best summarize the problem with an explanation of how most preachers—probably including you—were taught to preach. Respectable seminaries teach students how to make a grammatical-historical analysis of a passage. Seminaries that are a cut above the rest also teach something about literary and (even) rhetorical analysis. Those that excel, in addition, teach students to analyze the preaching portion according to the rubrics of systematic

---

[2]Jay E. Adams, *Preaching With Purpose* (Grand Rapids: Zondervan, 1982). The thesis of this book is that much preaching has failed because preachers have neglected God's intent in the preaching portion, using the passage for their own purposes instead.

and biblical theology. What they learn, at best, looks something like an incomplete pyramid. These analytical efforts, as you can see from the diagram, lead only to the *meaning* (an interpretation or exposition) of the passage.

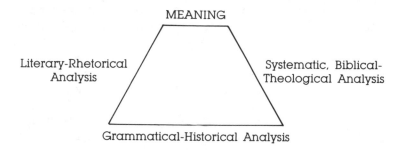

MEANING

Literary-Rhetorical
Analysis

Systematic, Biblical-
Theological Analysis

Grammatical-Historical Analysis

Having done all the work cataloged above, the result of which was meaning—an understanding of what the passage is all about—the preacher's task is to preach "academically" (lecture about) this *meaning*.

But this approach leaves the preacher with a serious problem: the pyramid is incomplete. His work was truncated just at the point where the final effort should have been made, where the *complete* meaning of the preaching portion would have been disclosed. The final step in the analytical process, neglected for so long, does not ignore the other analyses but uses them as a base to support a final analysis; that is their *raison d'etre*. The capstone on the analytical pyramid is *telic analysis* (see next diagram).

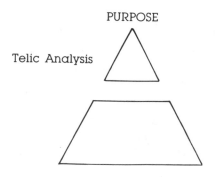

PURPOSE

Telic Analysis

It is almost as if someone attending his own birthday party were to remark on the decorations; study the ingredients, measurements, and texture of the cake; inquire about the significance of the number of candles on it; examine the wrappings of the presents; discover where each was purchased and how much it cost; count the guests; record all their names; and go away without eating any of the cake, ice cream, nuts, or mints, leaving behind all the gifts—virtually having "missed" the party by being caught up in every aspect of it except its purpose. That's what happens in nonapplicatory, non-telically oriented preaching.

Preachers, taught a lecture stance rather than a preaching stance, talk *about* the Bible (and subjects in it) rather than about God and their congregations *from* the Bible. Accordingly, they have been taught to look for "a central idea" or "theme" around which to build a sermon. But rather, efforts to analyze the preaching portion should uncover the purpose of the passage: what the Holy Spirit intends to do to the listener from it. Then, building the sermon on that, they should make the purpose of the sermon the same as the Holy Spirit's purpose in the preaching portion of Scripture. Preaching should not merely pack heads with truth; in John's terminology, it should enable people to "walk in the truth." That will happen when sermons are marinated in the *telos* of a passage.

In Isaiah 55:10–11, God likens His Word to the snow and rain. These have a *purpose*, which they *achieve*. They

> water the earth and make it bring forth and bud and so
> give seed to the sower and bread to the eater (BERKELEY).

So, too, the Scriptures have a purpose that they achieve:

> So shall My Word be, which goes forth from My mouth; it
> shall not come back to Me uselessly, but it shall do what
> I purpose and accomplish what I commissioned it
> (BERKELEY).

Even though God declares that His Word will be effective, accomplishing the purposes for which He sent it, that does not relieve preachers of their responsibility to proclaim that

Word. God makes His Word effective through the "fool-
ishness of preaching," (1 Cor.1:21) and asks, "How shall they
hear without a preacher?" (Rom. 10:14). God's determina-
tive will does not remove human responsibility; He has
planned that the Word will be effective in accomplishing His
purposes *through* preaching and not apart from it. He
therefore holds us responsible for becoming workmen in the
Word, workmen who "won't be ashamed, handling the
Word of truth with accuracy" (2 Tim. 2:15).

Clearly, portions of Scripture from which preachers
preach should be viewed in terms of the purpose for which
they were given. God intends to use His Word to accomplish
His various purposes. It is, therefore, the principal task of the
preacher to discover the purpose in his preaching portion
and preach it *in order to accomplish* what God *commissioned* it to do.

Telic analysis, properly done, leads to telic preaching
that is, by its very nature, applicatory. As Jefferson says,
when you preach "practically" you preach for life changes
in the members of your congregation. You do not preach for
the benefit of God or the angels (though, ultimately,
preaching and its results should glorify God by effecting His
purposes and pointing to His grace) but for the benefit of the
congregation of God's people assembled in His Name. That
is what preaching is all about.

APPLYING APPLIED TRUTH

Consequently, it is accurate to say that preaching is
truth applied. That means that the truth God revealed in
Scripture came in an applied form and should be reapplied
to the same sort of people for the same purposes for which it
was originally given. That is to say, truth should be applied
today just as God originally applied it.

Truth was not given in the abstract. Given in applied
form, God's truth should be preached in an applied form.
The apostles did not *preach* doctrine as a system but to
convey God's saving and sanctifying grace in Christ. When

you preach truth the way it was revealed, the entire sermon will be applicatory in effect.

Let's take an example. Philippians 1:27–2:13 forms a unit. The Philippian church was split by two quarreling women, Euodious and Syntyche (cf. 4:2–3). Before confronting this division head-on, Paul laid a groundwork for such a discussion by writing about unity and how to attain it. Because he was in prison, personally unable to come to their aid, he urged the church to listen and heed his words just as if he were present (1:27; 2:12).

Paul taught that concern for others would bring unity. Then he gives us the prime example of One who did just that: Jesus Christ. He who was in the very form of God, adulated by all the host of the heavens, did not think that the outward form of His deity was something to be held on to at all costs, but, *putting others before Himself*, He laid aside that glorious form and, instead, assumed the form of a slave. In human form He died for our sins the ignominious death of the cross. Because of that, God exalted Him and gave Him the name "Lord." So, says Paul, because I can't be with you, work out your own salvation (solution to this problem) with great care, guided by the principle of putting others' interests before your own (2:12), the way Jesus did. And in doing so, remember that you are not really alone: God is there working in and through you (2:13).

Certainly this section, containing some of the highest doctrinal teaching regarding the deity and incarnation of Christ, presents truth (doctrine) *applied*. Paul's concern is not to teach doctrine as such. But he does teach it—*for a purpose*. He wants believers to adopt the same attitude ("mind") that Christ had when, for the sake of others, He laid aside His own prerogatives. In emptying Himself of His glory (not His deity) and in humbling Himself, He demonstrated the attitude that, alone, could bring unity to the divided church. In order to achieve that goal, Paul taught doctrine. He knew that until they realized how much Jesus laid aside, how far He humbled Himself, they could not know what Jesus' attitude was like, and, therefore, could not understand what he meant. Life must be lived for Christ, according to sound doctrine (cf. Titus 1:1). But the doctrine in the passage (and I have only intimated it here) is given for a practical purpose; it is not taught academically. It is *truth applied.*

This means that doctrinal truth should be preached as practical truth and forcefully applied to people who divisively put themselves and their own interests first in the congregation.[3] He wanted doctrine to humble, shame, and guide them, bringing them to repentance and newness of life in Christ. Application brings Christ into the center of a message as the One who makes the difference in life.

A UNIFIED AIM

In *Preaching With Purpose* I wrote,

The preacher . . . using a genuine preaching outline applies all along the way; indeed, in one sense the whole sermon is application. The preaching format is an applicatory format by nature.[4]

In applicatory preaching there is no need to think about how to apply any given portion of the sermon. The entire sermon should be aimed at one and the same objective: achieving the *telos* of the passage. The combined weight of all the parts of a sermon should be brought to bear on the congregation as *one* powerfully combined application of God's truth. The sermon is the vehicle by which God today applies the same truth given long ago.

I spoke earlier of sermons that had application scattered about, sermons that go nowhere in particular, each section of the sermon an end in itself. Such sermons are like a tree, with each section like a branch.

One reason why sermons like this have little effect is that they lack concentration of purpose. On the next page is a sketch of a tree. Turn the page upside down and look at the tree. It has become a river, with all movement in one

---

[3]That is not to say, however, that there are not appropriate times for referring to the doctrine in Philippians 2 in a secondary way, *as doctrine*. But this should be done in a class on Christian doctrine, not in a sermon.

[4]*Preaching With Purpose*, 54.

direction, concentrating its power in one main stream. Each "branch" has become a "tributary" that adds depth, width, and force to the one river that rushes with ever-increasing power to its end.

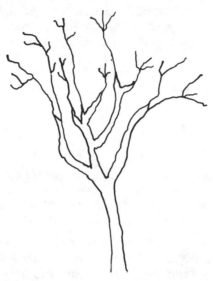

The "tree," with its dissociated points (branches), each ending in distinct applications that hang like so much fruit from the end, has now become a mighty force, flowing inexorably toward its destination. That is what happens when the whole sermon becomes the application of one great scriptural truth. Everything in the sermon contributes to a unified purpose, so that, like pressure applied to a wound, the sermon makes forceful contact that achieves its purpose.

When I say that preaching is truth applied, I mean that the truths of a passage are not merely expounded; they are so expounded (applied) as to effect change in the listener. Preaching turned into historical harangues, doctrinal dissertations, or exegetical exercises is no longer preaching. Someone has said, "Preaching is interpretation, not a mere repetition of the text." That is true, but that statement does not go far enough; preaching is application, not a mere interpretation. Calvin said:

. . .if we leave it to men's choice to follow that that is taught them, they will never move one foot. Therefore, the doctrine of itself can profit nothing at all.[5]

Calvin believed creeds should lead to deeds. Maltbie D. Babcock once said,

People have told me that they like my preaching because I do not preach doctrine. I do, but I cover up the dry bones and do not let them stick through the flesh, nor let the ugly skeleton show.[6]

The "flesh" that covered "dry bones" was a powerful application.

Biblical preachers so apply truth to the congregation that the people can no longer be the same for having heard it. They will change—for good or for ill (as God's Word accomplishes the sovereign purposes for which it went forth). Some may grow angry, others may repent, but, regardless of what it may be (depending on the heart condition of each listener) preaching-as-application *will have an effect*. When the apostles preached, things happened. When we preach today, there are such meager results. When you preach in an applicatory manner, there will be fewer of those noncommittal comments at the door ("Nice sermon today, pastor." "Enjoyed the sermon, pastor."). Instead, you will begin to hear comments like the following: "That really met a need." "I'd like to talk further with you about this message, pastor." "You rubbed the fur the wrong way today, preacher!"

Massilon, a famous French preacher, used to say,

I don't want people leaving my church saying, "What a wonderful sermon—what a wonderful preacher." I want them to go out saying, "I will do something."[7]

---

[5]John Calvin, *Sermons on the Epistles to Timothy and Titus* (Edinburgh: Banner of Truth Trust, 1983), sermon on 2 Timothy 4:1–2.

[6]Maltbie D. Babcock, *Fragments That Remain* (New York: Revell, 1907), 214.

[7]Quoted in Maxwell Droke, *The Speaker's Handbook of Humor.* (New York: Harper & Row, 1956), 111.

There is a place for lecture, for teaching facts in a more abstract way, in courses and classes, but not in the pulpit when you ought to be proclaiming God's Word in order to accomplish the purpose for which He sent it.

Let me conclude with the wise words of James W. Alexander:

> I still find myself trammelled, whenever I undertake to go in any of the regular harness of sermonizers. To be worth much, a sermon must begin like a river, and flow, and widen, and roughen, and deepen, until the end; and when it reaches this end, it is hurt by every syllable that is added.[8]

Taking Alexander's words seriously, I will refrain from adding another syllable to this chapter.

---

[8]James W. Alexander, *Thoughts on Preaching.* (Edinburgh: Banner of Truth Trust, 1975), 22.

4

Abstracting the Application

"So far, what I have read seems helpful, but the basic question remains—How do I apply to *my* congregation a message that was originally delivered to people centuries, or even millennia, ago? The times and circumstances are so very different. What does nomadic Israel in the desert have to do with a business man in this high-tech era, a so-called post-Christian period in which there lingers only the vestigial remains of two thousand years of Christianity that in its various forms has influenced the thought and life of Western men and women for good or ill? How do I bridge the gap between then and now?"

The problem is not new; Paul faced the same question in his day. The Corinthians considered themselves a "modern" society on the cutting edge of all that was happening in the Hellenistic world. Because they might think that Paul's references to Israel in the wilderness were irrelevant, he wrote:

> Now these events happened to them as examples and were recorded as counsel for us who live at the end of the ages. (1 Cor. 10:11)

On that basis, he applies passages about "nomadic" Israel directly to the Corinthian church. How could he do so?

Obviously, as Paul points out, the Scriptures were written for posterity. The events recorded about Israel, for instance, were not recorded for the sake of the Israelites whose bodies were scattered in the wilderness. In Romans 15:4 he makes the same point:

> Whatever was written before was written for our instruction.

In both passages, Paul's point is that the revelation given to Israel in the desert or in any other circumstance ("whatever was written") was aimed at his generation. Surely, Paul did not mean his generation alone but all those to come—including his. The writer of the Book of Hebrews, similarly, applies David's words to his day (Heb. 4:1–11). So, then, there may be more to any given portion of Scripture than at first meets the eye.

Paul believed that events recorded in the Bible were capable of being used as "examples" and as "counsel" and "for instruction." That means that they were designed not for one era alone but for the church in all ages. That much is evident. Paul had no problem preaching or teaching from the Old Testament Scriptures, even when speaking and writing to Christians, most of whom were Gentiles. Evidentally he knew how to bridge the gap. But how did he and other New Testament writers do so?

Let's consider his use of the Old Testament. We'll begin with 1 Corinthians 9:7–11:

> Who serves as a soldier at his own expense? Who plants a vineyard and doesn't eat its fruit? Or who shepherds a flock and doesn't drink some of the milk?

So far, by his three simple illustrations, Paul establishes the principle, acknowledged by all, that a person enjoys the fruit of his labors. Now, turning to the Old Testament to support his claim, he continues:

> Am I speaking from a human viewpoint, or does the law say these things? It is written in Moses' law, "Don't

muzzle an ox when it is threshing." It isn't about oxen that God is concerned, is it? Isn't he really speaking about us? It is written for us, because when the plowman plows and the thresher threshes he should do so in hope of having a share of the crop. If we have sown spiritual seed among you, is it too much to expect to reap material benefits from you?"

And, he continues in this vein, making his point that the laborer is worthy of his hire.

Now, examine the passage a bit more closely. Here Paul takes a command from Deuteronomy 25:4 that has to do with oxen and applies it to preachers, making the point that the preacher should live (be paid) from the work he does. How did he get that from Deuteronomy? Some would say that you can't get here from there!

Well, one thing is clear. Paul saw more in the Deuteronomy passage than many exegetes see. There is no indication that Paul read anything into the passage. No, exactly not that. His argument for paying preachers for their work comes from and is *founded on* the passage. How?

Paul saw in the Deuteronomy passage a principle that applied to oxen but also to all sorts of work situations, of which oxen threshing grain was only one example. Indeed, as he points out, God's main concern was not for oxen—that would be too narrow an interpretation of the passage—but rather, by the example of the ox, he wanted to set forth the general principle that the laborer should reap the fruit of his labors. The fact that this biblical principle applied even to oxen (arguing from the lesser to the greater) all the more indicates that it applies to soldiers, to farmers, to shepherds, and, preeminently, to preachers, who sow spiritual seed.

PAUL'S METHOD

Paul's method is to abstract a principle from a biblical passage and then apply it to a similar situation in his time. In doing so, he must do two things:

1. He must abstract the principle.

2. He must abstract the elements in the contemporary situation that approximate those in the biblical account.

When the elements in both the biblical and the contemporary situations match, the abstracted principle may be reapplied. In this way, the preacher can easily move from the one to the other. In it all, Paul was concerned with the *telos*, or purpose, of the biblical command. Note the telic question, "It isn't about oxen that God is concerned, is it?" Of course, God was concerned about oxen (cf. Jonah 4:11); Paul never for a moment intended to say that He wasn't. His question, however, indicates that God's concern extended far beyond oxen and that the exegete who fails to see this misses the whole point. The regulation concerning oxen was used to *exhibit* the principle; not to *limit* it. And, as I have noted, it is a pecularily good example because it shows the breadth of the principle, whose scope even included so lowly a creature as an ox.

The interpretative issue, then, has to do with *application*. It is not as if the preacher has to "find" situations to which to apply a passage. No, the principle comes, not as an abstraction, but as an already-applied principle. God set forth the principle in terms of oxen; that is, He gave us the truth applied. Therefore, it is the preacher's task to discover the principle operating in his preaching portion. When he does so, he will learn not only the general, abstract principle, but how God has already applied it. Then he must preach the principle in his own context, to the people before him, applying it to them, exactly as God applied it when first revealing the truth.

THE BROADER PRINCIPLE

The principle that a worker should make his living out of his work lay behind the command "Don't muzzle the ox." That principle applies broadly to all workers in every sort of legitimate work. The strong language Paul used in rejecting any narrow application of the principle to oxen alone shows that he considered it not only wrong to do so but eminently foolish. It was wrong to do so, not only in New Testament times, but from the first. Moses never intended any such thing. From the days of Moses on, the principle held, *and it should have been understood and applied as broadly as necessary*. Paul did not misuse the Mosaic passage; he rightly applied it.

To apply truth, then, is to use it to achieve the same *telos* as the one originally intended: to inculcate and apply the principle in the same way by particularizing it to a given instance. The applicatory similarities are found both in the *telos* of the passage and in the *telos* of the message and in the elements in the situations (then and now) to which the passage applies.

God's purpose in recording the things that were written was not to supply us with information that we might apply as we see fit. That, unfortunately, is the course on which the Puritans set the English-speaking world so many years ago and from which it has never veered. No. God shows us how to apply His Word by doing so Himself *in the giving* of the truth. He communicated truth in applied form. It is not your job to search out possible applications for truth but to uncover those situations in our time and place *to which it already does apply*.

Does this mean that there is one truth but many applications, as some have said? Well, yes and no. If we take it to mean that all sorts of possible applications regardless of the abstracted principle behind the one applicatory example in a passage, then, no. But if it means that the principle, as it was originally given was intended by God and the writer of Scripture to apply to a whole range of situations like the one to which it was applied when given, then, yes. The question is not "What *did* it mean then and what *does* it mean now?" but "What does it mean—in any time or culture?" To what sorts of situation is it always intended to apply?

In bridging the gap, avoid the endless discussions of "meaning" and "significance." Instead, look for the original intent, the *telos* of the passage, and abstract that in terms of a principle. Then find what is common to both the biblical and the contemporary situations. For example, in the record of Jesus' washing the disciples' feet, ask what was *intended*. What is the purpose of His command to us to do as He has done? Did He institute a ceremony to be observed? With all due respect to those who believe so, their interpretation is like those who limited the Deuteronomy 25 passage to oxen. No, Jesus was setting forth a principle, the import of which is that, in love, we should be willing to serve our brothers and sisters by performing even the most humble sorts of tasks. That principle might extend to bathing a bed-ridden, incontinent Christian who needs your help, or to doing any number of other menial tasks one might ordinarily shy away from.

Let's consider another passage: Galatians 3:1ff. In this passage Paul is upbraiding the Galatians for turning back to Judaistic ideas, he writes:

> Galatians, you are stupid! Who has put a spell on you, you before whose eyes Jesus Christ was placarded as the crucified One? Tell me this one thing only: did you receive the Spirit from works of law or from hearing with faith? Are you really so stupid? Having begun by the Spirit are you now going to be completed by the flesh?" (Gal. 3:1–3)

Now the whole discussion had to do with Judaism. Judaizers followed Paul all over the Mediterranean world, telling his new converts that their faith was incomplete, that they must be circumcised and keep Jewish feasts and ceremonies in order to be saved. Paul strongly counters all such teaching in this emotional and powerful letter. His indignation at the charge that the gospel was insufficient appears throughout. In these three verses we see it in his choice of language. But how will a preacher today preach from this passage? Surely, in very few cases will he encounter Judaistic tendencies! There will be few members of his congregation, if any, throughout his entire ministry who will be tempted to defect to Judaism. Is the passage passé? Has it nothing to say to

Christians today? Of course it does! It is as up-to-date as your morning newspaper.

All around are cults, abberations of the faith, legalistic and moralistic teachings within the church itself that well-meaning, but foolish Christians are tempted to adopt. These fall under a general principle that God gave his church through Paul in this applied situation. The principle is clear: You must grow in the Christian faith, not by moralistic or legalistic works (works done in your own strength), but rather by completing your Christian life as you began it. You didn't regenerate yourselves; it was the Spirit who gave you life to believe. He gave you your new heart. You didn't manufacture it yourself. So, then, if you want to grow, you must grow by the work of the Spirit in your life, as He produces His fruit (chap. 5). Your own unaided works are dead and can only do harm. This principle can be applied broadly to all sorts of situations in which legalism threatens Christian growth.

Consider another. In 1 John 4 we are told to test the spirits. Not every belief comes from God. How may we do so? Well, says John,

> by this you know God's Spirit: every spirit that confesses that Jesus Christ has come in the flesh is from God, and every spirit that doesn't confess Jesus isn't from God. (1 John 4:2–3)

And so, again and again you read in Christian literature that *the* test for uncovering false doctrine is whether a teacher denies the incarnation of Christ. But many cults and false religions accept the incarnation. For example, Mormons believe that Jesus Christ came in the flesh. Are they acceptable, therefore? No, there is something wrong in this teaching about testing the spirits. What is it, and how can we correct it?

Once more, the approach to application that we have been taking comes to our rescue. We will look for a broader principle behind his statement. John was writing in a context. The problem was incipient Gnosticism of the sort that said Jesus' body was a phantom or that the Christ came on Jesus at the baptism but left Him before the cross. In either case, the problem was a denial of the incarnation. So, John's letter is truth *applied*.

But is there a broader principle? Definitely. And it is the universal test for distinguishing truth from error:

> We are of God; whoever knows God listens to us, but whoever isn't of God doesn't listen to us. From this we know the spirit of truth and the spirit of error. (1 John 4:6)

John himself sets forth the broader principle that, in his situation, applied to gnostic views of the body as evil. This teaching was not according to the inspired apostolic Word and was, *therefore*, error. The test is whether or not a teaching is in accord with apostolic teaching, which is found in the New Testament. That principle, clearly stated by John, applies to all sorts of situations today.

The Book of Proverbs is a gold mine of applied principles. Here one finds a wealth of life experiences that illustrate these principles. But the principles are bigger than the proverbs themselves. When the reader is warned against removing a boundary marker (22:28; 23:10–11), surely the principle affirmed is that you should not alter fact or circumstances to your advantage, thereby cheating another. This principle is broadly applicable to all sorts of relationships in society (or in the church) that have nothing to do with boundary stones as such. As you can readily see, the principle is taught, not abstractly, but as truth applied.

In the parable of the Good Samaritan, where we are exhorted to "go . . . and do likewise," Jesus doesn't restrict us to the helping of injured pedestrians who have been robbed. What is taught is that we must help those in need even if they are not "our sorts" of people. Our "neighbors" are not restricted to some narrow group, as the Jews believed, but consist of anyone whom God brings into contact with us. Widely applied, the principle behind the parable has clear application to our times.

AN EXAMPLE TO CONSIDER

Let's look at an example of such applicatory preaching:

> "Prophylaxis" may be a technical term, but it stands for practical truth. To guard against perils is better than subsequent attempts at remedy or consequent pains of remorse. God told His people of old that when they built their flat-roofed houses, on which many an hour would be spent, they must build a battlement. If they did not, and any one fell off, his blood would be on the owner's head.
>
> Ought we not to put guards at points of peril in our lives—not for others alone, but for our own exceptional moments? We are not always at our best. We are not always safe where ordinarily we move without peril . . . railings are better than ambulances, and building parapets than setting bones? Looking for springs of evil is a better investment of time than groaning at the mouth of a muddy river; and preventing the sowing of the seeds of sin, than taking care of harvests of shame . . . who shall refuse, though he be strong and steady, to build battlements at dangerous edges of his life, lest a weaker brother may fall where he stood safe?[1]

Now, the preacher in this sermon has the right idea. He may have strayed a bit too far away from the principle when he says we should apply to ourselves a verse that manifestly teaches concern for the welfare of others, but he returns to the principle when he begins to talk about the example of one's life to a weaker brother—quite an interesting application of the principle. Clearly, the principle applies to putting fences around swimming pools in neighborhoods where children might fall in and drown, but does it not also apply to our concern for weaker brothers? Who would have thought of that at first glance? Yet the principle, it seems to me, is altogether in keeping with the New Testament emphasis in which teachings about Old Testament sacrifices

---

[1]Maltbie D. Babcock, *Thoughts for Every-day Living* (New York: Scribner, 1914), 96–97.

are applied to the sacrifice of one's life in Christ's service and to prayer.

"But isn't that taking license with the Scriptures? Can't you use passages to prove nearly anything on that basis?"

I share your concern, but I must be faithful to the methods exhibited by New Testament preachers. Plainly the process of application that Paul follows can be abused. There are dangers, to be sure. But a good thing must never be rejected because of the danger of misuse. You don't stop using knives because some have carelessly cut themselves, and others have used them to commit murder. Rather, you insist that they be used with care in proper and safe ways. In spite of that, some will always misuse knives. That is not your responsibility. You must use them well and, to the best of your ability, help others to do so.

The same is true of the biblical process of preaching. Just as one may learn to use knives in careful and responsible ways, so too he may learn the safeguards that, if followed, will keep him from straying into applicatory areas not actually covered by the principle behind the passage from which he is preaching.

I will list several questions that you must answer satisfactorily if you want to properly apply biblical principles to your congregation:

1. What is the *telos* of the preaching portion? Is that also the *telos* of your sermon?

2. In what sort of situation does the *telos* occur? What was going on? To what is it addressed?

3. In the passage, who is doing what about the situation
   a. to understand it?
   b. to change it?
   c. to complicate it?

4. How does God view the situation? Is He
   a. pleased with it?
   b. displeased with it?

5. What response does He require?

In answering these questions, you will be able to abstract both the principle that is applied in the passage and the elements in the situation to which God applied it. With both in hand, you will be able to apply the passage to life today in a way that approximates it in its essential particulars.

A passage is not rightly interpreted until it is rightly applied. Interpretation is not merely what God meant in the specific biblical instance to which a principle was first applied; it also includes the application of the general principle, applied now. It is doubtful that an interpreter understands any given passage unless he can rightly show how that passage may be applied to a modern congregation.

With the understanding of application that we have just been setting forth, it is easy to see how you may bridge the gap. And when you do, you will be able to preach as John Calvin did when he said over and over again in his sermons words like "Paul commands us here . . . ," "The Holy Spirit tells us. . . ." Calvin preached the Bible, not as a book of history that occurred long ago and far away, when God used to do things in the lives of His people, but as a contemporary book, written to his congregation. Your task is really quite simple, in spite of all the pages written that have complicated the question. What you must do is discover the truth taught in any passage, extract from it the general principle of which the preaching portion is an example, then see how God applied it, and do the same. That, in a nutshell, is the preacher's task.

5

The Holy Spirit and Preaching

The Holy Spirit is the great Preacher. He is, therefore, God's Applier of truth. And He still preaches today—through those He chooses, commissions, gifts, and enables to preach His Word, the writing of which He so carefully superintended.[1] The Holy Spirit intended the Bible to be given for the benefit of the church of all ages (Rom. 15:4; 1 Cor. 10:6, 11). He continues today to work through that Word as it is preached (see, e.g., 1 Cor. 2:4–16; 1 Thess. 1:6; Heb. 3:7; James 1:21; 1 Peter 1:11–12, 23, 25; 3:18–19; 2 Peter 2:5).

Now if it is true that the Holy Spirit is the Great Preacher and is intimately connected with the proclamation of the Word, then it would be interesting to know His views on preaching. What does He consider important? What are His

---

[1]See Jay E. Adams, *How to Help People Change* (Grand Rapids: Zondervan, 1986), chapters 12, 14, for biblical argumentation that the Holy Spirit preaches through preachers who faithfully proclaim His Word. The Bible indiscriminately attributes the same acts to the Holy Spirit, the Scriptures, and the minister of the Word in such a way that the only conclusion one can reach is that the Holy Spirit enables the preacher to perform those acts by means of the Scriptures.

concerns about various aspects of preaching? Is this a hopeless quest, or is there a way to find out something of what the Holy Spirit considers faithful preaching?

Interestingly enough, there is. Unfortunately, few people recognize this fact. But if such information exists, it would be negligence of the highest order to ignore it in any study of applicatory preaching. Therefore, we will take the time to investigate the matter by a somewhat circuitous route, and at the end of our search we should have uncovered some important information.

INSPIRED PREACHING?

In Acts 2:4, 14 an unusual word occurs (the only other New Testament use of it is in Acts 26:25). It is the Greek word *apophthengomai*. This term means to proclaim in a clear, loud utterance under miraculous influence. It was used by the Greeks to describe the utterances of oracles and seers. In the Septuagint it is used of prophesying (cf. Deut. 32:2; 1 Chron. 25:1; Ezek. 13:9; Zech. 10:2). Perhaps the best translation of the word in the Acts passages is "to speak out in revelatory words under inspiration."

What does this mean? It means that Peter preached a sermon inspired by the Holy Spirit. Is this unusual for the apostles? No. It was expected, because Jesus Himself promised them that they would do so. Consider the following passages:

> But when they deliver you up, don't worry about what you will say or how you will say it, because what you must say will be given to you in that hour. You aren't the ones who will be speaking, but the Spirit of My Father speaking in you. (Matt. 10:19–20)

> Now when they arrest you and bring you to trial, don't worry beforehand about what you will say. Rather, say whatever is given to you in that hour (it won't be you speaking, but the Holy Spirit). (Mark 13:11)

> Don't worry about what to say in defense or how to do so, because the Holy Spirit will teach you in that very hour what you ought to say. (Luke 12:11–12)

> Get it settled in your hearts not to practice your defense beforehand because I will give you words and wisdom that none of your opponents will be able to withstand or contradict. (Luke 21:14–15)

Now, what do these passages say? Simply that in the crucial hour, when everything depends on what is said, the apostles will be inspired by the Holy Spirit in such a way that their responses will be His responses. They will be as inspired in preaching the Word as when they write it.

I realize that all four quotations refer to arrests, court trials, and so on. But as the Book of Acts indicates, these also were events used by the Spirit to proclaim the truth through His apostles. The "defenses" were, in fact, offenses for the gospel.

Why, then, didn't the Lord promise that they would also be inspired in ordinary preaching situations? It seems that He focused on the more dangerous circumstances because He wanted to encourage the apostles about them. His promise doesn't exclude inspired preaching on other occasions. Indeed, the use of *apophthengomai* in Acts 2:4, 14 clearly indicates that the apostles were enabled to preach inerrantly on other occasions as well. And note also that the same word is used by Luke to describe the inspired preaching of Paul *during a trial* (Acts 26:25). There is a clear correspondence here between revelatory preaching at trials and preaching on the Day of Pentecost. Moreover, Jesus promised inspiration to the apostles on two other occasions:

> The Holy Spirit . . . will teach you everything and will remind you of everything that I told you. (John 14:26)
>
> But when the Spirit of truth comes, He will guide you into all truth . . . and He will tell you things to come. (John 16:13)

These two promises do not relate to trials. However, although they surely have to do with the writing of the Scriptures, there is no reason to limit them to that; they could every bit as well refer to the apostolic Word, inerrantly proclaimed, prior to its inscripturation and final incorporation into one Book. Here is a promise that the Spirit would teach things both old and new. It seems comprehensive, indicating that all they needed to know would be given to them. Timothy Dwight, in his sermon XLIX, says that

> each inspired man was, as to his preaching, or his writing, absolutely preserved from error.[2]

Now, in all of these passages the intimate connection of the Holy Spirit with preaching is evident. And when you consider the insight into the Old Testament prophecies that Peter and Paul displayed in their preaching, you recognize that more than the man was at work in the sermon.

Indeed, in a valuable but little-known book, Stiffler puts it this way:

> But when Peter's address on this morning is studied, we have still more convincing proof of the Spirit's presence. In its adroitness, in the arrangement of the arguments, in its analysis, in its steering clear of Jewish prejudices, in its appeal and effect, it is without a peer among the products of uninspired men. As an example of persuasive argument it has no rival. The more it is studied, the more its beauty and power are disclosed. And yet it is the work of a Galilean fisherman, without culture or training, and his maiden effort. The analysis is perfect. . . .
>
> In marshalling these arguments there is great skill. The theme, The Messiahship of Jesus, which, of course, was in Peter's mind from the first, is not announced until the very close of the address. To announce it at the start is to secure its scornful rejection at once, or at the very least to awaken prejudices that will harden the mind against the arguments in favor of it. But at the close it comes in irresistibly, supported by all its proofs. Who taught the provincial fisherman this bright piece of oratorical wisdom? How was it that when he first mentions the distasteful name of Jesus he calls him a "man," and does not declare him to be the Christ until he has proved him such? What guided him so that he

---

[2]Timothy Dwight, *Theology Explained and Defended in a Series of Sermons*, vol. 2 (New York: Harper and Brothers, 1854), 137.

did not at the start turn the attention of his hearers from that wondrous phenomenon which had won and held them—the speaking with tongues? Again, the order of his threefold argument shows masterly skill. His first one is drawn from the acknowledged facts of Jesus' life—"as ye yourselves know." His second is from the Scriptures. His third from the wonder now before them, the gift of tongues. He puts the strong argument first, the one least appreciated, because most difficult, in the middle, and the most impressive one last. Who taught the unschooled Peter this perfection in argumentation?

Again, how did Peter miss the pitfall of the novice in not making in this address a great deal of his own personal experience? . . .

Pages might be written on the grandeur of this address, which, it must not be forgotten, was extemporaneous. But this is sufficient to show that he who wrote it was either under supernatural influence, or was a supernatural person. To deny the inspiration of the address is to cast us on the other horn of the dilemma, that Peter was mortal man. It does not relieve the question much to say that Luke or any one else put it in Peter's mouth. For then Luke, or that other supposititious person, must be more than mortal. The structure of the speech transcends human power. It must have come from God's Spirit.[3]

"Well, all of this is most interesting, but what has it to do with my preaching?" you ask.

I told you I was going to take a circuitous route in coming to an answer to that question. But we have now finally arrived.

If the Holy Spirit inspired the sermons in the Book of Acts, then two important conclusions follow:

1. The study of the sermons in the Book of Acts will yield many principles from which we may learn what the preaching that the Holy Spirit desires is like.

---

[3] J. M. Stifler, *Introduction to the Study of the Acts of the Apostles* (New York: Revell, 1892), 18–22.

2. The promises of inspiration, since they refer to preaching, indicate those elements about which the Holy Spirit has special concern.

Since this is not a book on preaching in the Book of Acts,[4] we will look most carefully at the second conclusion.

THE SPIRIT'S CONCERNS

In summarizing the things that the four major promises amount to, one might say that the Spirit will give them

the right thing to say ("what"),
in the right words ("how"),
in the right way ("wisdom"),
at the right time ("in that hour").

Here, then, are the things that seem to matter to the Holy Spirit: content, language, manner (approach), and timing.

Content cannot be discussed here beyond saying that everything the apostles preached was scriptural. It was either an exposition and application of Old Testament truth or a proclamation of new truth that would, in time, become part of the New Testament. Both of these elements are also set forth as the sources from which Timothy (and preachers today, to whom he was told to pass the torch) must preach:

You, however, must continue in the things that you learned and are convinced of, knowing from whom you learned them.

That is the apostolic Word, preached by Paul and the other apostles that, today, is found in the New Testament. Paul continues:

and that from childhood you have known the sacred scriptures.

---

[4]Roger Wagner, a capable doctoral candidate at Westminster Theological Seminary in California, is working on a text that will study preaching in the Book of Acts in depth. There is no need, therefore, to develop that theme in this volume.

That, of course, is a reference to the Old Testament. Paul then says:

> All Scripture is breathed out by God and is useful for teaching, for conviction, for correction and for disciplined training in righteousness, in order to make the man from God adequate, to equip him fully for every good work. (2 Tim. 3:14–17)

Applicatory sermons, then, are based solidly on the Scriptures of the Old and New Testament. All a person needs for carrying on a ministry of evangelism and edification is contained in those Scriptures. This was to be true not merely in Timothy's day but down through the ages (cf. 2 Tim. 2:2).

The right words are mentioned as the second concern of the Holy Spirit. Clarity and boldness are involved in this, as Paul indicated in Ephesians 6:19–20 and Colossians 4:3–4. Under the heading "Applicatory Language," I have said much about this matter that need not be replicated here. With reference to boldness, as such, let me mention a thought or two. The word is one of two terms used in the New Testament for boldness. This word, *parresia*, means, literally, to speak freely, unencumbered by fear of consequences. Probably more preaching in our time is hindered out of concern for what Mr. Jones will think or how Mrs. Smith will react to it, than by any other factor. I will not develop the theme of boldness, because I have done so already in another volume.[5]

I would be remiss if I did not mention the preacher's prayer—one that you probably ought to pray before every sermon—found in Acts 4:24–30 (note especially verse 29): the apostles prayed for boldness to speak God's Word fearlessly. As a result, we are told,

> Now as they were praying, the place where they were meeting was shaken and they were all filled with the Holy Spirit and spoke God's Word boldly. (Acts 4:31)

---

[5]Jay E. Adams, "Preaching to the Heart," in *Essays on Biblical Preaching* (Grand Rapids: Zondervan, 1983), chap. 5.

If more preachers were to pray this prayer, more congregations would be shaken! Preaching today is utterly tame when compared with those sermons in Acts.

The Holy Spirit is concerned about preaching done in the right way: with wisdom. Chapter 11, entitled "Applicatory Knowledge," deals with this issue. Wise preachers know their congregations, the problems they are facing, and the best way to approach them. Chapters 6 and 8, "Applicatory Introductions" and "Applicatory Examples," also deal with the matter to some extent.

Finally, the Spirit wants the right thing spoken, in the right words, in the right way, *at the right time*. This refers to timing, more specifically to a readiness to present the message that is needed *when it is needed*. It was "in that hour" when the apostles would be "given" what they needed. Their messages would, therefore, be timely.

INSPIRED PREACHING IS APPLICATORY

Now, what do the Holy Spirit's four concerns about preaching amount to? Just this: He is concerned about applicatory preaching. The content for the trial, the words for the trial, the approach at the trial, and the timing of it all relate to those who would hear the message. The Holy Spirit wanted the gospel to be powerfully brought to bear upon those who heard it. All of these spiritual enablements were given to help apostolic preachers forcefully apply the message to those who heard. That is the purpose of applicatory preaching.

What the Spirit told the apostles *not* to do (to consider beforehand what they would say) is precisely what you *must* do, because your preaching is not inspired. In forbidding them to prepare their speech in advance, He implied that the ordinary and proper means of preparation, apart from the extraordinary gift of the Spirit, is to give careful thought beforehand.

I commend these four concerns of the Spirit to you. They are matters about which the rest of this book has a great deal to say. It would be interesting to study each of these sermons in the Book of Acts from these four perspectives. Although that is not possible here, you may wish to make such a study on your own. But, at least, if as a matter of course in preparing your sermons and in evaluating them afterwards you will focus on these four factors, your preaching will soon improve. After all, what the Holy Spirit thinks is important you too should consider important. There can be no more signifcant fact for you to understand than this: *The Holy Spirit has made known His concerns about preaching.*

6

Applicatory Introductions

Some sermons start slowly, amble along, and begin to pick up momentum only when it is time to close. I propose, instead, that you begin strongly, continue vigorously, and end aggressively. Applicatory preaching will enable you to do so. But you must begin properly—or all is lost.

One sermon I studied recently consisted of sixteen pages of fairly small type. It took the reader fifteen of those pages to reach the preacher's first applicatory comments, which, to my chagrin, occurred only in the final paragraph.

The all-too-common practice of tacking on applications at the end of a sermon runs counter to biblical preaching. In this chapter I want to show you how to open your message with application—in the introduction!

"How do you do that? I don't understand."

I am sure that this is the response that comes to the minds of many of you. Let me assure you that there are many ways of making introductions applicatory. But I will concentrate on just one that is clearly biblical and, when developed and followed, will take you a long way toward changing dull, routine preaching into preaching that your congregation will call "vital."

APPLICATION FROM THE BEGINNING

Let me suggest that you *preach out of an event.*

The first two sermons in the Book of Acts were in the fullest sense occasional. That is to say, they arose out of and were addressed to an audience at a given occasion or event. On Pentecost the coming of the Holy Spirit, with all the outward effects that accompanied it, brought together a crowd of curious and interested listeners:

> "They were astounded and amazed . . . saying to one another, 'What does this mean?' " (Acts 2:7, 12)

This curiosity provided the introduction to Peter's message.

On a second occasion Peter spoke to a crowd that was already eager to hear him. At that time it was the healing of the cripple at the temple gate that drew them:

> So they were filled with amazement and astonishment at what had happened to him . . . all the people were amazed and ran together to them (Peter and John) at the portico called "Solomon's." (Acts 3:10–11)

And later Paul at Lystra and at Athens found himself addressing audiences already curious about his mission and anxious to hear what he had to say.

In each of these instances, the introduction to the sermon was an event. It was an applicatory introduction that led to the most important experience of the listeners' lives.

Wouldn't it be great if every week, when you rise to preach, you have before you a crowd of people already stirred to the marrow? People primed to hear what you have to say?

"Sure, that would be great. But such events don't take place every week in my congregation. In fact, few things ever happen that pique my congregation's interest. If they did, I could preach with more enthusiasm and people would listen more eagerly. Certainly there would be better results."

I think you are right. As a matter of fact, in my book

entitled *How to Help People Change*, I compare and contrast teaching in the counseling context with teaching in the preaching context, pointing out that

> the counselor has one great advantage over the preacher: the counselor teaches in the milieu. . . . Teaching in the milieu, addressing the actual situations people are facing, makes a great difference."[1]

But what is the difference? The counselor, like Peter and Paul, teaches the counselee about matters he already considers important to him. That is to say, a counselor speaks to the counselee about something that has already captured his interest and concerns him. Indeed, it may be all-engrossing. To put it another way, counseling begins with an applicatory event.

Like the concerned counselee, Jews who had gathered on Pentecost were asking, "What does this mean?" (Acts 2:12). They were already shaken to the roots. And it wasn't long before they were asking, "What should we do?" (Acts 2:37). In a sense, the movement of an effective sermon may be described by the change in concern expressed by these two questions. Curiosity and interest at the outset should give way to a desire to learn and do God's will. Good preaching always satisfies both of these concerns.

"But," you ask, "how can I bring this off? I don't have events like Pentecost happening prior to each sermon!"

Of course you don't. As a matter of fact, you don't even have the starting advantage of the counselor who addressed his words to a present concern of the counselee. That makes it more difficult for you.

Naturally, on those rare occasions when the president is shot, the Christian school bus overturns, or the oldest member of your congregation is beaten and raped, your people will want to hear a word from God about these events. You must not disappoint them, leaving them only with the slant on the event that they get from the media. But,

[1]Jay Adams, *How to Help People Change* (Grand Rapids: Zondervan, 1986), 83–84.

fortunately, such events do not happen every week—as you rightly point out.

You begin with the most difficult task of all. You must speak week by week to people who are often apathetic, whose concerns are elsewhere, who see no immediate application of the passage of Scripture from which you will preach. It is not an easy task to capture their minds, create concern, and begin applying God's truth already in the introduction.

CREATING AN EVENT

How, then, is it done? The answer is both simple and complex—simple in that it is easy to say, and complex in that it takes time, thought, and effort. The answer is: *You must create an event.*

"Create an event? What do you mean? Am I to stage some happening or something like that? Surely you are not advising theatrics, are you? I don't understand. You'd better explain."

God seemed to think that this was a good way to open a sermon, because He used it so frequently in Acts to prepare audiences for the apostles' messages. Every counselor knows how much easier it is to interest a person in a biblical passage when its message bears on a recognized problem in his life. That is why the wise preacher creates an event for the members of his congregation at the outset. He does not presuppose that people who have been thinking all week about something else will be interested immediately in what he has to say. He knows that he must capture their attention, stir them out of lethargy and indifference, and move them from other interests to the matter at hand. And he must get them so interested and concerned before he actually begins to deliver the message, as such, that, like the Jews on Pentacost, they will be asking for more The best way I know to do that is to create an event.

The "event" I am talking about is not an objective event occurring in time and space. Rather, it is subjective, occurring in the mind, creating a mental milieu. Properly described, however, such an event can be just as real to those who listen as if it were actually happening. When someone cries "fire!" in an auditorium, the concern and the resulting action of the audience may be exactly the same whether there is an actual fire or not. Only one thing is necessary to get action—it must be convincing. The same is true of preaching. When Whitefield, Spurgeon, and Edwards spoke, people became so involved that they gripped the pews for fear, reached out to keep someone from falling over a cliff, got up to man lifeboats, etc. These preachers verbally created events to which their congregations responded.

That is what you must learn to do in the introductions to your sermons. Time and thought must be given to discovering how best to involve the congregation in each truth you proclaim. Sometimes it will require description of the sort used by the preaching greats mentioned above, sometimes it will be something less dramatic.

"But I'm not a Spurgeon, Whitefield, or Edwards!"

No, of course you aren't. One reason why may be a lack of effort in developing your descriptive powers. That requires a willingness on your part to do the hard work of preparation that they did. The biggest problem is not a lack of native ability or God-given gifts, it is simply that you do not take the time necessary to create a verbal event.

"If I were to make the effort, how would I go about it?"

Let me suggest these guidelines to begin with:

1. Do not begin with the text; begin with the congregation as Peter and Paul did. Turn to the passage of Scripture only when you have adequately oriented your congregation to what they will find there and only when you have sufficiently stirred up in them a concern to know about it. Acts 2:12 must precede Acts 2:37.

2. Take enough time to create the mental event. Sometimes it is not necessary to say much, as screaming "fire!" indicates, but usually it is. Many preachers prematurely terminate introductions that are heading in the right direction. While there is nothing worse than a poor introduc-

tion dragged out, a good idea aborted before it is born is not much better. So when you have worked hard on a good introduction to your sermon, take time to include enough detail for the congregation to visualize the situation. Usually, it takes more than two sentences to bring that off. More often, you will find yourself speaking several short paragraphs. But let me warn you that filler, unnecessary repetition, and all other dead, inert content must be brutally excised.

3. Learn how to describe events. Practice telling stories on other occasions. Work on using vivid, concrete verbs and nouns. Tape and listen to others who are adept at description. Analyze what they do to discover their techniques.[2] Then incorporate the principles you discover in your sermons; don't copy theirs. Write out introductions, choosing the key words and phrases you plan to use. Be sure to include these in your full-sentence outline *(supra).* You can learn to create an event, if you will only put sufficient time and effort into it.

4. Test the introduction before using it. If you cannot feel (I mean physically feel) the effects of what you are saying *in your body,* then it is not going to do the job. Keep working on the introduction till you feel in yourself the concern, the excitement, the fear, the anticipation, or whatever the introduction ought to create. When you can describe the event in a way that sends a chill up your spine as you do so, you are on the right track. If the introduction doesn't grip you, it won't grip the congregation either.

Why should sermons be boring or dull? Certainly apostolic sermons were not! Sermons are dull because preachers make them dull. Think about it: every passage of Scripture is *God's* Word. Your job is to so describe the problems that people face and the solutions that Scripture gives that listening to God's Word becomes important— nothing less than an event! Indeed, *the* event of the week.

---

[2]For a method of analysis, see Jay Adams, *Sermon Analysis* (Denver: Accent, 1986), part 1.

APPLYING THE EVENT

Now you must apply this event in some way to the lives of your people. It may apply either directly or indirectly. You may begin by saying something about the congregation itself:

> In this congregation there are serious problems that must be addressed. This morning I propose to mention two and tell you what God wants you to do about them.

Then, as Jesus did in the seven letters of the Book of Revelation, you proceed to address the state of the congregation from an appropriate preaching portion of Scripture. That is *direct* application in the introduction.

Here is another, somewhat more extended direct applicatory introduction:

> Some of you are in trouble. In a congregation this size and in a world of sin and problems, that is certain. How are you handling it? Some of you have just emerged from a period of trouble. How did it go? Are you battered and bruised, broken and defeated? You say, "I can't remember when I was in trouble last." Well, then, look out for Thursday—trouble is probably waiting right around the corner.
>
> If trouble is all that common, you must learn how God expects you to handle it. Some of you may not handle it all that well. Some people cave in under trouble—they go all limp, like a rag doll that the stuffing has been knocked out of. Others get angry and blame everyone around them for their trouble. They kick the dog, say things they later regret, and generally make themselves unpleasant. Still others sit in the corner and hold a pity party for all who will attend. Clearly, none of these responses is biblical.
>
> "I can see that," you say, "but how does God expect me as a Christian to handle trouble?"
>
> God has answered that question in the words of the apostle Paul found in Philippians 1:12ff. Let's turn to that passage and see what He says. . . .

Surely you can see how these two *directly applicatory introductions* involve the congregation by their very content. The direct applicatory introduction is, perhaps, easier to compose and use than the *indirect* applicatory. Yet it is not always the more effective. The passages in Acts that record God-given events that served as introductions for apostolic preaching, were indirectly applicatory. That is to say, those who gathered to hear did not understand *from the outset* that they would be intimately involved in what was happening. All they knew was that a very strange event had taken place, and they were curious to know more. The apostles had to *relate* their message *to* the event that occasioned it, showing how it was of the utmost importance to those who listened. Involvement in the first place, then, was the involvement of curiosity. Having caught their attention by the event, the apostles had to hold it by their explanation of the event. It is necessary when using indirect application, to say, with Peter, "This is that" (Acts 2:16).

Let me read you an example of a powerful, indirect introduction:

> I know you have had it happen to you just as I have had it happen to me: someone comes up to you and tells you that one of your dear friends has suddenly become seriously ill.
>
> "Did you hear about John?"
>
> You look at the questioner and you know that something shocking is coming. You wait for the briefest of seconds before the answer comes, and in that millisecond, you know that your life will be changed by the answer.
>
> "John has cancer." Or the answer might be: "John had a heart attack this morning." Or: "John had an accident."
>
> "Oh, no!" you say. And then you ask for details. What kind of cancer is it? A heart attack—how is he doing? How bad was the accident? Is John going to live?
>
> Oh, those are horrible moments! Depending on how close the person is to you, you experience different degrees of shock, dismay, and despair. "I hope he

makes it through—I hope he lives"—this is what you think, or you say it to your friend who is telling you the bad news. You shake your head. Possibly you feel tears forming. You look away and wonder where you can go to pray for his recovery.

That is the event. Unless you are a hard-hearted, insensitive person who cares for no one but yourself, you *must*, of necessity, be drawn into the event, anxious to learn where the preacher is going. He has got to you. But can he hold you? That is where the bridging step from the event to the listener must do the job. Here is how Joel Nederhood, the preacher whose event is quoted above, continues, drawing you into the message:

Now, it's happening to John. But sometimes it happens to us ("you" would have been the more powerful word here). Maybe you've experienced this. "Well, what do the tests say, doctor?" you ask. It's three right on the dot, Thursday afternoon—he had told you, "Call me around three on Thursday, and I'll know more." You try to keep your voice calm, as if you are asking the time, but your stomach is in knots and you are tense because you know that if the news is bad, your life will never be the same.

The doctor hesitates on the other end of the line, and then the words come: "It's malignant; pathology says it looks like a . . ."—he says one of those obscure words that refer to one of the tumors we human beings get. "I'm sorry. But it could be worse. We've had some success in treating this. We'll have to run some more tests. I'll be in to talk with you tomorrow."

And that is that. That is everything. That changes everything. Nothing is as it was five minutes ago. The message has come to you: You are sick, and you have a disease that could kill you; in fact it might kill you.[3]

Powerful! Effective! He caught you—didn't he? Notice how he personalized the introduction from the first sentence on by using the second-person pronoun *you*. But also notice

---

[3]Joel Nederhood, "Good News for the Sick," in Jay Adams, *Sermon Analysis* (Denver: Accent, 1986), 213.

how, in two stages, Nederhood draws you into his net. First, you are the listener, receiving bad news. The mood is created, the tone is set. Yes, you can see yourself standing there listening to the report about John. You can feel yourself empathetically responding to the bad news. Your curiosity is piqued. Having spread his net and having coaxed you onto it, Nederhood suddenly draws the net, and you find yourself swinging inside: "Now, it's happening to John. But sometimes . . ." A masterful stroke! You are caught. You must now consider what God wants you to do when, at "three on the dot," the doctor says you have cancer. That is a two-stage, indirect, applicatory introduction, par excellence. Can you see it?

When using the slightly delayed, indirect, two-step introduction before the message itself, the preacher must convince the people of his congregation that the message is of vital importance to *them*. It is not enough to create the event. The indirect, applicatory introduction demands more—the second step: bridging the gap from the event that creates curiosity to concern about some aspect of the listener's own life as he applies the point of the event to himself. Interest alone is not enough; the introduction must be applicatory. Because they involve two steps, rather than one, indirect applicatory introductions usually are more drawn out and take more time to develop. Be careful not to cut them short.

STICK TO LIFE TODAY

Introductions that have to do with matters long ago and far away rarely do what Nederhood did for his listeners. The congregation cannot bridge the gap to their own lives. Therefore, ordinarily it takes an introduction about something contemporary to help them understand why a biblical passage should be of such great importance to them today.

Sitting in front of you are people who have practically severed their marriages during the past week, people whose children are threatening to shack up with dope addicts, people who are concerned about cancer, people who are about to collapse under the strains of caring for an infirm, elderly parent. When they settle down to listen to a sermon, the introduction of which indicates that they will probably receive a 30–40 minute discourse on the Amalekites, they will turn you off before it is finished. You have to either give them the word of comfort, encouragement, or warning that they need, or create an event that you make so significant that, for a time, they are willing to lay aside other concerns to hear about it, or you will lose them. They are not going to listen to a sermon that threatens to be a dull lecture on what God *used to do.*

But please notice, I am not saying that a sermon from a passage having to do with God and the Amalekites could not bring hope, comfort, or instruction about how to face life's trials. No. But if you intend it to be more than a lecture on what happened long ago in Palestine—when God *used* to do things in the lives of His people—then the introduction should surely signal that fact by the way in which it applies to the members of your congregation.

People will not only put up with details about what happened long ago, but will fairly relish them when they know *from the introduction* that these details are important to an understanding of how God will work in their lives during the coming week. In other words, the introduction should *orient* the congregation to what to expect of the sermon.

THE INTRODUCTION ORIENTS

Indeed, intended or not, the introduction always does orient the congregation. When the preacher says nothing about his listeners in the introduction and promises no help or direction for today but begins with the text, focusing his remarks on the past alone, regardless of his intentions, he is telling his congregation that they are going to receive a lecture *about* the Bible rather than a message *from* the Bible *about* themselves. If and when the preacher gets around to applying his data to them later on in the sermon, many will have already tuned him out, and he will find that it is too late to woo them back.

In other words, applicatory sermons are preached from this side of the Atlantic. Always stay at home when preaching. Begin in America, take your stance firmly on good old American soil, and, except for brief excursions to Palestine to explain a passage *in situ*, keep your feet firmly planted on the ground where you live. And on every trip to the Holy Land that you must take, be sure that you bring your congregation home. There is always the danger of leaving them behind. But there is an equal danger of turning your message into little more than a Holy Land tour of the text. Remember, you are not a tour guide; you are a herald of the King.

So then, applicatory introductions begin with the congregation rather than the text; this will help them understand and appreciate the message from God to follow. In the sermon the Bible will be no less in evidence, but it will be clear that you preach from the Bible rather than lecture about it. You will preach the Bible as a Book with contemporary messages for your congregation. I call such introductions "applicatory" because from the outset people know that the Bible will be applied to them. Indeed, when the introductory event so captures the listener that he wants to hear more, he will eagerly accompany you to Palestine, oriented not only to what the trip is designed to uncover, but to bring back what he learns to transform his life. And that's the purpose of preaching!

SAMPLES TO CONSIDER

Let's look at a couple more introductions—one good, one bad. After the first, we'll look at its excellencies. Then we'll take a look at the second and determine how we might rework it. Here is the good one:

> One week ago a very presumptuous announcement
> appeared in our church bulletin. It declared that Holy
> Communion would be held. How could we be so sure?[4]

What makes that a good introduction? A number of factors.
But note especially that it is applicatory in almost every
sense of the word. Apart from the use of the first person
("our," "we"), it meets all criteria (he might have said "your
church bulletin" and that "today you would receive Holy
Communion"). First, it creates a problem—an event. Not a
very dramatic one, like the Pentecostal event, or even the
event with which Joel Nederhood's sermon began. But it is a
problem that could be of some importance. The words
"presumptuous announcement" along with the question,
"How could we be so sure?" serve to raise an issue. They
disturb one's equilibrium. He wants to know, "What is the
preacher getting at?" Those ominous-sounding words are
calculated to shake up lethargic souls who might otherwise
mechanically receive the Lord's Supper. But they are of such
a nature as to make even zealous attendees take pause.
There is an implied warning that things might not proceed
according to schedule; something may go wrong. That is
creating an event.

Moreover, the preacher sends a clear signal to his
congregation that the message will be contemporary. He is
preaching in America, not on the shores of some Mediterranean country. This will be no lecture about the past: it has to
do with the very service in which they are about to
participate. The Lord's Supper will be served—but will
communion be held? That is the question.

And there is even more than a slight hint that the
answer to the question he has posed will depend on the
congregation. In some way, what he is going to say so
deeply applies to them that they will determine whether the
announcement was accurate or not. They have an immediate stake in this message!

In three short sentences, this introduction succeeds in
creating an event. Compared to the healing of a cripple, it

---

[4]Lloyd John Ogilvie, *The Cup of Wonder* (Grand Rapids: Baker, 1976), 95.

is a mini-event, but an interest-arousing, concern-engendering event nonetheless. It is a serious event, with a serious outcome; there is an implied threat and promise.

Now, look at a typical nonapplicatory introduction that causes no event to occur (the listener responses are mine):

> Nicodemus is well known. His story has often been told. ("If so, why tell it again?") We study here the beginning of his Christian life. ("Oh, great! So Nicodemus was a notable man; what's that got to do with anything?") It is fashionable to speak slightingly of his coming to Jesus by night. ("Who cares?") It is sometimes said that he was cowardly. But this may not be a fair criticism. ("What difference does it make? The Lord knows the truth.") Night may have been the best time when he could hope to find Jesus free for an undisturbed hour's talk with him. ("Hmmm . . . I wonder when John and I will ever get an undisturbed hour to talk over the problems with our kids. . . ." (She's lost. But the preacher drones on.)) We must read the story through to the close to see if the subsequent mentions of Nicodemus confirm the charge of timidity or cowardice in him. We shall find that just the reverse is true. . . .[5]

And on and on it goes.

What's wrong with this introduction? Everything! First, the congregation is nowhere present in it. It begins with an assumption that the people gathered before the preacher can't wait to hear whether Nicodemus is a coward or not. This may be a burning question to the speaker, but his interests are surely different from the average listener's thought, which I interspersed!

Preachers who think as this one did need to ponder the sign that was on H. V. Kaltenborn's desk when he was the managing editor of the *Brooklyn Eagle*. It read: "Always

---

[5] I do not care to reveal the source of this introduction since I attack it and the sermon so severely. I will simply say that the preacher is now with the Lord. His faults were not his alone, however; all of us at times have fallen into the same traps. Surely it is profitable to become aware of the problems involved in order to learn to do something about them.

remember that a dog fight in Brooklyn is more important than a revolution in China."

The introduction announces that the focus of the sermon will be a "study" of Nicodemus' "Christian life." Why would the preacher take valuable preaching time to do that? Such an announcement points to a lecture about the past. It is clear that this lecture will be *about* a Bible character, not about God and the people gathered in the church building. The introduction is an introduction to a lecture on the Bible, not a sermon from it. It is not applicatory.

Can we do anything to help? Can it be retrieved? Well, consider the rest of the message that followed this introduction. The preacher wandered through the story of Nicodemus, eventually making one brief exhortation or another. No *telos* (purpose) of the Holy Spirit in putting the story there was ever disclosed. The sermon was like a tree rather than a river. Let us sharpen the focus, therefore, by concentrating on one element: the necessity of a new, spiritual birth for entrance into the kingdom of heaven. How might the preacher have involved the congregation from the beginning? Consider the following:

> You will not make it. You simply don't qualify. Oh, I know you have a strong Christian heritage, you have been baptized, you attend church regularly, you give to good causes, and you call yourself a Christian. But you won't make it!
>
> You may be a Sunday school teacher, a deacon or elder—it really doesn't matter. The fact is, you won't make it. You won't go to heaven, regardless of all this—unless you are born again.
>
> That's what Jesus told Nicodemus, a Jewish religious leader who—if you were to total up his religious acquisitions—would probably far outshine you. But Jesus told him, just as He now tells you: unless you are born again, you will not see the kingdom of God.
>
> Because of the crucial importance of this matter, let's be sure you make no mistake about it. This is no place for a slip-up. Otherwise you could end your days here in

false security, only to find yourself consigned forever to the company of that large number of scribes and Pharisees who thought they would go to heaven but now suffer in hell. Let's turn to John 3 to hear what Jesus has to say to you about the new birth.

Can you see any difference?

"Yes, of course. But you rewrote it entirely."

Certainly; there was no other way. As I said, *everything* was wrong—the content, the approach, the audience analysis behind it, etc., etc. Sometimes the only way for you to redeem a sermon is to simply rethink and revise those sections that need it.

I did not search for either of these two examples. They were both taken from books that happened to be lying on my desk at the moment. Yet they serve admirably to make my point. The particular way in which I rewrote the second introduction is certainly not the only way that it could have been done. There are many possibilities. But with very little effort (I spent only about five minutes to revise it) you can turn a nonapplicatory introduction into one that is much more likely to grab the congregation—once you understand how to do it. Why not take a few of your old sermons and practice improving your introductions (as needed) in a similar manner? After you've puzzled over two or three, you will begin to get the hang of it.

One way to begin revising an introduction is to look at what you plan to talk about in the conclusion or toward the end of the message. Usually, if you have been following the older methods, you will discover applicatory material at this point. Turn that material inside out and upside down. Bring up later solutions to problems in the introduction as questions to be asked, problems to be solved. Turn later imperatives into questions, resolution of tensions into tensions, how-tos into "hows?" and what-tos into "whats?" Then introduce this inverted material at the outset. Use the second person freely, working hard to introduce it in the first sentence, if possible. Make it explicit—in one way or another—that this sermon will deal with the lives of those seated before you.

We have seen that how you begin is all-important. It may entirely prejudice your listeners for or against you. It will either involve them or lose them to other more pressing interests. While they may not be able to articulate what is wrong if you lose them, they will sense it, saying under their breath, "We're in for another dull lecture (although they'll probably mistakingly call it a 'sermon')." So take time to develop the skill of creating an event. Practice until you are good at it. You will soon discover the difference it makes in the expectations and participation of those who listen.

In conclusion, let me sum up. An effective, applicatory introduction consists of at least four essential elements:

1. An event that grabs and tightly holds the listeners' attention, making them want to hear more. Usually the event will be "mental," created by the preacher.

2. Involvement of the congregation in the event. If the introduction is direct, the event itself, when effective, *involves.* In such cases, point 2 is superfluous; nothing more must be done. If it is indirect, the preacher must show his listeners how the event is important to them.

3. A personalized introduction, using the second person, "you." Try to use "you" in the first sentence if possible.

4. A promise, explicitly or implicitly made, that the sermon will be from God's Word about the congregation and their relationship to Him. Then—keep the promise!

7

Applicatory Format

Of all the aspects of applicatory preaching, perhaps the principle that the whole sermon is application is most apparent in its organization.

Of course, the outline of a message (unless it contains something of significance to the congregation) exists for the benefit of the preacher. Its function is to keep him on course, to aid his memory, and preserve the message in a retrievable form for possible later use. Therefore, the outline should not be announced.[1]

It is in the message format that a preacher's true theory and practice of preaching can most clearly be discerned. When discussing how he preaches, he may say much about many things, but what he actually believes about preaching most plainly appears in the way he finally organizes his materials. Those preachers who understand that preaching is application organize their points for application.

To begin with, look over an outline (yours or someone else's) to see whether there is dynamic unity of the sort

---

[1]For the argumentation on this point, see Jay E. Adams, *Preaching With Purpose* (Grand Rapids: Zondervan, 1982), 53, 55–56.

exemplified by the ever-widening, deepening river or the static disunity exemplified by the tree. Scan the introduction to see if application begins there, then let your eye flow down the heads and subheads of the outline to see if it continues throughout. In this way you can readily distinguish an applicatory sermon from those that are not.

If there is a purpose (telic) statement at the beginning, you should immediately turn to the conclusion to see if the two approximate each other. If in the purpose statement the preacher says, "My purpose is to bring hope to people in grief," and in the conclusion you find him doing nothing more than arguing for a certain eschatological viewpoint, you know that he got off the track somewhere in the body of the sermon. (If your objective is Los Angeles and you end up in Las Vegas, somewhere en route you made a wrong turn.) Scan the outline backward from the conclusion to find where he took the wrong turn. In this way, by playing one part of the sermon over against another, you can soon determine whether the outline is of a piece—an outline that is likely to produce an applicatory sermon.

For an analysis of the whole, particularly when you are looking for unity, it is hard to improve on the analysis of an outline. Why not dig into the barrel and try this out on some of your own outlines?

Conversely, to achieve all the objectives alluded to in the previous paragraph, it is necessary to know how to construct outlines that apply God's truth. Of greatest importance is properly framing the applicatory points (or heads).

TWO IMPORTANT MATTERS

Before we look further, let me suggest two things:

1. Set out at the top of the outline (after the title, and before the introduction) the *telos* or purpose of the sermon;[2]

2. When composing an outline, use complete sentences.

---

[2]Ibid., chap. 1.

Let's consider each of these, beginning with the second. Sometimes thoughts that are so vivid at the moment you first conceived them that you believed you would never be able to erase them, fade after a time. Yesterday's "unforgettable idea," or your way of expressing it, may have become today's vague impression. Incomplete sentences—phrases, key words, etc.—may not afford adequate help in jogging your memory. The full-sentence outline, on the other hand, is always there to do so.

Moreover, until you can express a thought in sentence form, you may not have it entirely clear in your mind. Often we fool ourselves into thinking we have a tight grasp on a truth when our minds may only be lightly fingering it. Forcing yourself to state a point in sentence form usually exposes the problem, thereby helping you to avoid that trap. This is significant, because vague thinking results in obscure, fuzzy, muddled preaching.

Setting out the purpose of the sermon in an initial purpose statement (again, in full-sentence form) does several things:

1. It forces you to see if you know (and can clearly articulate) the objective of the message. Unless this is clear to you, all else will falter.

2. It uncovers unsuspected dual (or even triple) purposes. Often sermons lack unity because the preacher is trying to move in several directions at the same time. The purposes compete with and defeat one another. In such cases, either subordinate points (one or more of the tributaries) have been wrongly placed parallel to the mainstream, when they ought to feed into it, or you really have too much material for one sermon. If the latter is true, one or more of the competing purposes will have to be laid in your sermon seed bed until a separate sermon grows from it.

3. The telic statement helps you stay on track when composing each point of the outline. Keeping the *telos* in mind *when setting out the heads* of the sermon enables you to be sure that everything that goes into the sermon contributes to its end.

But now let's return to the points themselves. They

should be "applicatory points," points that by their very nature and structure *at every state* carry home the message to the listener. Were they to be announced (which is not advantageous unless there is a good reason for doing so), they themselves would speak to the congregation in an applicatory manner. Let's consider the following outline:[3]

A More Excellent Way
(1 Corinthians 12:13)

That is the title. Here is the outline for this sermon on love:

I. Its Ministry of Healing
II. Its Simplicity of Language
III. Its Competency for Problem Solving
IV. Its Superiority of Value

That is lecture outline, not a preaching outline! It is structured in such a way that, if the preacher follows it, he will be lecturing about love rather than preaching to people. It is abstract (note that all the second and fourth words in each point are abstract), and it is impersonal. This outline is not designed for application. Nothing about the points themselves is applicatory. Try to preach one of them; you can't.

Can this sermon be "translated" into a preaching format? Yes, by simply making each point applicatory. Here are two possible suggestions for doing so:

I. Your Love Can Heal
II. Your Love Can Speak
III. Your Love Can Solve Problems
IV. Your Love Is Important

or

I. God expects you to heal others by love.
II. God expects you to speak to others by love.
III. God expects you to solve problems by love.
(Eliminate point IV as not really a part of this message.)

Clearly, the two suggested "translations" differ from the

---

[3]T. T. Crabtree, ed., *The Zondervan 1983 Pastor's Annual* (Grand Rapids: Zondervan, 1982), 22–25.

first in several important ways. They are personal (the congregation is addressed in second-person language throughout): in each point the message is applied to the listener, it is concrete, and is a complete sentence. Indeed, if you were to speak any one of these sentences in the sermon itself, you would be preaching to the people of the congregation about themselves from the Bible in relationship to God and their neighbors. Note also that the *Annual* outline calls for a lecture: the four "Its" point back to love as an abstract quality. In contrast, both "translations" preach!

Can you see the difference? When you follow the last two outlines, they will keep you preaching to your congregation throughout the sermon because they are in applicatory format. You will move from one obligation or opportunity of love to another (the sermon might be entitled along those lines: "What Your Love Can Do" or "What God Expects of Your Love"), always keeping the members of the congregation in mind as those who must show love, those to whom the message is sent, and, therefore, those to whom and about whom the preacher must talk.

Let's consider another outline in a lecture format.[4] See if you can "translate" it into a preaching format in the space provided:

Lecture Format (John 3:16)	Preaching Format
I. Its Costly Expression	I.
II. Its Unworthy Object	II.
III. Its Saving Purpose	III.

How did it go? Did you find it difficult? Well, it will take a while to catch on. But, perhaps I can make a few suggestions that will help. One way to move from a lecture format to a preaching format is to include the words "God" and "You" in every main head. Now, go back and try that out. It helped, didn't it? That isn't the only way to go, of

---

[4]In James Daane, *Preaching With Confidence* (Grand Rapids: Eerdmans, 1980), 70.

course, but it is one good way. It might be wise, when beginning, to use it regularly.

Sometimes you may wish to eliminate a point (as I did in one of the "translations" above); at other times, you may want to change the order of the points. There is no reason for always following the order in which points may appear in the preaching portion. Let's consider an outline in which you might put the last point first. Here is the outline as given:[5]

I. The Spirit within
II. The world without
III. The Spirit overcomes

Of course, you must first "translate" the outline into a preaching format. Then, in order to hold the hope of victory over the world before a defeated people *from the outset,* you may wish to reorder the points:

I. You can defeat the world
II. By God's Spirit within
III. Battling the world without

However, you may wish to retain the order:

I. By God's Spirit within you
II. You can face Satan's world without
III. And win the battle

Note in the last two outlines how the three points form a continuing idea. That is one way to assure that you have unity in your sermon. All three points become parts of one continuing sentence, interrupted only by the supporting exegetical and illustrative content subordinated under each. Play around with that. Write a sentence that can be broken down into two or more parts, about each of which you could say a good deal that is helpful, and make each part a point in your outline. Each part, in itself, may not form a complete sentence (though often some may), but all parts taken together do.

Well, after all this, it's about time for you to try your

---

[5]Crabtree, *1983 Pastor's Annual,* 131–32.

hand at it again. Here's another that you can try to "translate":[6]

Lecture Format	Preaching Format
I. The Fullness of Divine Forgiveness	I.
II. The Freedom of Divine Forgiveness	II.

Compare your "translation" with mine (see footnote 6).

Now, having practiced with the outlines above, why not seriously work on some of those sermons that you took out of the barrel? Doubtless, you will find many (if not all) of them written in the lecture format. See how easy it is to turn them into applicatory sermons, once you get the hang of it. And notice how great a difference it always makes. You will find yourself often omitting the last point—if you were one of those who relegated the application to that place—because you are already applying the material all along. Yet it is not so much that you apply as you go ("This is what God says to the Corinthians—and therefore to you"); rather, you apply *as you speak* ("Listen to what God tells you in 1 Corinthians").

An applicatory format enables you to say everything in an applicatory way. As a result, the entire orientation of your sermon is different. Because it will not be necessary to repeat so much, you will find that you have opened spaces for greater detail and more illustrative material. Thus, in one stroke, you will eliminate unnecessary repetition and preach in more depth, and you will begin to preach sermons that are vital to the congregation throughout.

---

[6]Ibid., 114–16. Here is my "translation":

I. God will fully forgive you
II. God will freely forgive you

Of course, there are other ways of saying the same thing. For example:

I. God will forgive you
II. God will forgive you fully
III. God will forgive you freely

8

Applicatory Examples

Application is closely related to the use of examples, illustrations, and stories. That relationship has to do mainly with the types of examples used. Fundamentally, effective preachers use examples for five purposes:

1. To clarify;
2. To demonstrate how something takes place;
3. To motivate (encourage and warn);
4. To make something memorable;
5. To prove or (at least) to support a viewpoint.

Often examples and stories are used mechanically rather than thoughtfully. For example, consider this advice: "Be sure to use at least one illustration for each major point and sometimes, if the subpoints are lengthy, for each of them as well." Such advice, all too frequently given, misses the mark.

While examples, stories, instances, and illustrations, told well, are intrinsically interesting and hold interest when sprinkled throughout a sermon, holding interest should never be *the* determining factor in deciding when to introduce an example. Preachers can legitimately consider the interest that examples provide as only a by-product. It is wrong, therefore, to think (as some do), "Hmmmm, this part of the sermon seems a bit dry. I'd better spice it up with an example or two."[1]

Illustrations should be introduced into a message when a point is cloudy, abstract (and thus hard to visualize in actual life situations), complex, or otherwise difficult to grasp. In such portions of the sermon, examples *clarify*.

> So, from what I have told you of Tom's experience, you can more readily understand what God is saying to *you* in this passage.

In explaining Ephesians 4:25, where Paul says, "Speak truth, *because we are members of one another*, a preacher might say,

> Paul is using the figure of the body to show that all the functioning parts involved in a bodily action must have the same true information if they are to coordinate properly. The hand must know what the knees know and vice versa. Otherwise, the hand may reach around and pull the chair out from beneath the body as the knees bend to make it sit down. There is too little coordination in the body of Christ because there is too little truth. That is why people are perpetually pulling the chair out from under you.

It is also incumbent upon a preacher to illustrate his point when people are having trouble implementing some biblical directive:

---

[1]Nevertheless, Luther's observation holds:
> The common people are captivated more readily by comparisons and examples than by difficult and subtle disputations. They would rather see a well drawn picture than a well written book . . . it is useful to have comparisons and examples on hand (Ewald M. Plais, ed., *What Luther Says*, 3 vols. (St. Louis: Concordia, 1959), 3:1129).

Luther's concern, you will note, centers on the "usefulness" of the comparison and example, not primarily on its interest value. Whenever one or more of the five purposes of examples listed above can be truly served, then choose an example rather than a comparison. That is where the interest value tips the scale.

As you can see from this story, it isn't enough to know *what* God wants you to do. If you want to please Him, you will have to learn how to turn doctrine into practice. From what you have learned from the episode with Mary and Bill, you can clearly see one way to begin.

You are preaching on the confession of sin—telling about the need of going to a neighbor, admitting sin, and seeking forgiveness. You want to make the point that in confession you must come clean, tell the whole story, and not shade the truth. Well then, you might tell the story of a farmhand who went to his employer and confessed, "Some time ago I stole a rope from you." The farmer freely forgave him. But the farmhand had no peace of mind. The problem was, he failed to mention the fact that on the end of the rope had been a horse.

Good preachers, then, use examples not only to clarify a truth, but to demonstrate how biblical injunctions may be *implemented* in daily living.

Sometimes illustrations are needed to *encourage* or otherwise motivate people to action. There is a sign at the "Narrows" in the Garden of the Gods, just outside Colorado Springs, where the road disappears into a narrow crack in a rock cliff—so narrow that it looks as though you couldn't drive a VW through it. But just as you are about to turn around, you spot the sign that says "Yes, you can—millions of others have." That's all the encouragement most people need. And often all that some of the members of your congregation need when they stand puzzling whether they can make it or not, is the encouragement that comes from hearing how others did it. In such instances, a story or two is much better than exhortation. Paul understood the principle plainly when be wrote 1 Corinthians 10:13: "No trial has overtaken you but such as is common to man." Good illustrations, like the one at the conclusion of the Sermon on the Mount, help to *motivate* (a problem most preachers face).

Then, of course, illustrations make truth *memorable*. Merely to mention the story of the prodigal son, the good

Samaritan, or the Pharisee and the publican is enough to bring the truths embodied in those stories to mind. By means of a memorable story it is easy to make truth so concrete that, once understood in that form, the story may even become a kind of paradigm for that truth.

And stories may even have *evidential* value:

> Now, I know this may be hard to believe, but let me tell you what happened when a husband got hold of this biblical principle and put it into effect in his marriage. Why. . . .

If you can give two or three examples of how a command was implemented in actual cases—especially ones known to those who are listening—those example take on the nature of proof.

"But how does application figure into the choice and use of examples?"

THE CHOICE AND USE OF EXAMPLES

The answer is probably obvious from what I have already said, but let me develop the point in some ways that may not be quite so obvious.

1. Application has to do with truth *related* to the listener. Examples that have to do with people in similar situations who have struggled with the same difficulties as the listener bring the herald's message down to earth. They convince people that God is interested in doing more for His people than packing their heads with facts to be regurgitated at the next Bible quiz. Wise preachers choose examples that describe life *as their people know it*, the way Jesus and Paul did. Jesus talked about Samaritans, the road from Jerusalem to Jericho, shepherds and sheep, women and dowry coins, and wayward sons. By means of examples like these, He, and all effective preachers after Him, have walked right up, knocked on their listeners' door, and said, "I have a message from God for you and your family."

2. Good preachers choose examples that are *appropriate* to the point being made. They carefully select material

that fits both in content and in tone. When talking about Christian zeal, they will choose the example that has to do with fire over the one that has to do with ice (unless they want a contrasting example, showing the opposite quality).

Jesus carefully crafted the motivational example with which he closed the Sermon on the Mount. Because it was designed to motivate His listeners not merely to *hear* but to *do* what He taught, He wanted to show the benefits of heeding His words and the dangers of failing to do so. So He developed a dramatic story that had to do with torrential downpours and floods. These *appropriately* paralleled the storms of life through which people must live. The collapse of one house and the endurance of the other during the storm aptly made the point that His truth alone, incorporated into life, lays a foundation solid enough to withstand trials. Trials, like storms, beat us down if we are not adequately prepared for them. Houses are like lives: the foundation on which they are laid is all-important. Foundations are like the principles and practices on which people base their words, thoughts, and deeds. The material and the tone of the story are both highly appropriate.

3. Effective preachers choose illustrative material that is simple and complete. They do not use illustrations that call attention to the illustrations themselves because they are so complex they are hard to understand, or so incomplete they cause people to wonder what happened next. It would be a mistake to try to attempt to clarify a point in a sermon by some esoteric principle of nuclear physics that would itself take time (and several illustrative examples) to explain. Yet some preachers, enamored with the illustration itself, do just that. Illustrations must be simple, easily understood, and readily applied. Moreover, they must be complete.

When teaching the use of dialogue in stories, I often illustrate the value of dialogue to the student by using an incomplete story. I describe a tenting experience one night in Estes Park, Colorado:

> It's 2 A.M. Suddenly, I am awakened by a scratching sound on the side of the tent—kraaaaatch, kraaaaatch!

Rousing my companion, I whisper, "Bill, Bill, wake up. . . . Do you hear that?"

"Huh?" he answers. "Go to sleep; leave me alone."

"No, don't roll over, Bill. Listen . . ."

Kraaaaatch!

"Aw, that's just a branch scraping the side of the tent. Good night!"

"But, Bill, it isn't. It's . . ."

And then I stop, leaving the story incomplete. Invariably, students want to know what happened next. "Nothing," I say. "That's as far as I need to go to show you something about dialogue and the use of nondictionary sounds."

"Yes, but was it a branch or a bear?—or what?"

"That's not important to my point," I tell them, stringing them along a little further.

"Yes, but it is to us!" they insist.

So, you see, I purposely let them down to show, in addition to my points about dialogue, that they must never do this to a congregation. Leave a congregation hanging on some unresolved aspect of a story and you will lose them every time. Not only will your illustration fail to illustrate, because it calls attention to itself rather than the point it was supposed to make, but it will also divert listeners' minds from the flow of the sermon. They too will wonder what happened next. You may never pull them back again. That is the peril of the incomplete story.

4. Effective preachers use illustrations *only when needed.* Donald Grey Barnhouse was a master of illustration. If you want to learn how to develop and use illustrations, especially personal illustrations, then study his sermons. But there are times when he overdid it. He often used several examples when one would have done the job. And I have found in one of his sermons from the Book of Romans an instance in which an illustration illustrates an illustration! That's going a bit too far. When your content is straightforward enough by itself, stories and illustrations only slow down the sermon. They tend to irritate the listener who has

already grasped your point and must now tread water while you drone on about something that is not all that enlightening or helpful. Avoid Barnhouse's tendency to use *too many* examples—especially two or three under the same subpoint, where one would do nicely.

Overkill happens for one of two reasons. Sometimes the preacher has two excellent examples and doesn't want to sacrifice either, so he uses both. At other times, he doesn't have any one example good enough, so he hopes quantity will make up for poor quality. Of course, it doesn't.

When using examples for proof, however, it will often be advantageous to use more than one case per point to show that the first example is not a rare or isolated instance. When using examples to demonstrate how to implement truth, more than one may be necessary to indicate that there are several ways to implement it.

DIALOGUE

I have mentioned dialogue and "nondictionary sounds." I teach my students that the Lord used dialogue even when He pictured the prodigal son *alone* in the far country. He has him talking to *himself!* Indeed, he describes him using quotes within quotes: "I know what I'll do; I'll return to my father and say to him, 'Father, I have sinned against heaven and you. . . .'" That's how important Jesus thought dialogue is in a story.

How do you know when to use dialogue? A rule of thumb is to use it whenever the story begins to have any significant length to it. If it takes more than four or five sentences to tell, you probably should introduce some dialogue.

Dialogue aids application significantly. It brings the story up to date. As you make people talk to one another, or to themselves in a story ("Now, let me see, where did they say the rip cord is?"), it is as if the event were actually going on at the moment. The reporter who uses indirect discourse ("The prodigal was hungry and determined to go home and ask his father to make him a hired servant") always places the event in the past. Dialogue has a present quality about it; it is as though you were hearing the conversation for the first time. To *involve* people, use dialogue; they are much more likely to vicariously experience the truth in this way.

"But what do you mean by this phrase you've been using—'nondictionary sounds'?"

When you feel free enough in preaching to use sounds that can't be found in the dictionary, you are probably getting somewhere. Novices rarely do—and seldom do very well. Let me give you a couple of examples. I have an illustration about a new tin garbage can in which I talk about the lid fitting perfectly—schunk! But after the garbage collectors have finished kicking the can around and backing over the lid with the truck, the lid will never fit again. Instead, the lid will go (here I make wobbling-type noise with my tongue, accompanied by an appropriate hand gesture, that I can't even reduce to paper). Such sounds, when done well, tend to enhance dialogue. You will hear them used all the time in stories told by the great storytellers like Garrison Keillor and Jean Shepard.

HUMOR

"What about humor? Your garbage-can illustration sounds as if it were a humorous one."

Right. There is a lot more humor in the Bible than many people realize. In the original languages there are humorous plays on words not reproducible in translation, and there are even puns! What *can* be seen by the average English reader, if he stops to think about it, is humor in illustrations. Take the use of exaggeration, for instance. Here is a man with a log sticking out of his eye trying to pick a speck out of his brother's eye. Here is someone straining gnats out of his soup, but swallowing a camel! Or, think of trying to squeeze that camel through a needle's eye! That is Palestinian humor used to illustrate a point. The very grossness of the exaggeration shocks, tickles the fancy, and makes truth memorable.

If you must choose between a humorous and a nonhumorous example, all other things being equal, *if it is appropriate*, take the humorous one every time. But be sure it *is* appropriate. Be sure it doesn't clash with the mood set by your content. Humor, for instance, doesn't usually go well with a discussion of the agonies of hell!

"Why does humor help?"

Well, as Mary Poppins sings, "A spoonful of sugar helps the medicine go down."

Consider two preachers illustrating the same point. The preaching portion is "Cast all your cares on Him; He cares for you" (1 Peter 5:17).

The first uses an illustration of a son dumping burdens out of his knapsack into his father's on a backpacking trip. It is a good, appropriate example. But dull.

The second tells of meeting a man who used to be the world's worst worrier, totally cured of his worries. He asks,

> "What's happened to you, Fred? You look as if you haven't a care in the world."
>
> "I don't."
>
> "That's great! How'd you get rid of all your worries?"
>
> "I hired a man to worry for me."
>
> "You did what?"
>
> "I said I hired somebody to worry for me."
>
> "Well, *that's* different! Say, what's he charge?"
>
> "Five hundred dollars a day."
>
> "Five hundred? Where are you going to get that kind of money?"
>
> "That's his worry!"

Then the preacher goes on to make his point: "Wouldn't it be wonderful if you could do that? Well, Christian, there is Someone who has offered to take all your cares upon Himself—and He won't charge you a cent."

Which illustration will better make the point? Which will be more memorable? Which is more likely to show how remarkable an offer God is making?

Used wisely, examples are a chief means of applying truth to life. The parables of Christ—often the sum and substance of one of His messages—clearly demonstrate this. It is literally true that Christ's sermon, at times, was the telling of a parable. Today it is rare to find preachers developing and using parables even as a part of their sermons.

"How could Jesus preach through a parable?"

It was possible because preaching, as we have seen, is *truth applied.* And that is precisely that a parable is: truth applied to listeners as it is embodied in the elements of a story aimed directly at them, as they are, in their situation. The story comes as close to being pure application as any other preaching element. It is, in effect, the application of truth in a situation paralleling that in which the listener finds himself. The elder brother *is* the scribe or Pharisee who grumbles over Jesus' mingling with sinners in order to win them. The two situations are identical—someone who has gone astray is reclaimed; the proper responses are the same (the shepherd, the woman, and the father rejoice); only the older brother is out of sync. Indeed, he is even out of sync with the angels of heaven.

One value of a story is that it can be concocted to fit exactly what you want to say. It is not necessary to use only true stories, so long as you don't try to pass off the fictional stories as having actually happened. There is flexibility here. You may alter a true story or manufacture one from scratch. All you must do is honestly indicate what you have done. You can do so by some simple introductory phrase like, "Suppose a person were to . . ." or "What I am talking about would be like a person who . . ." or even, "You have all met people who. . . ."

There are dozens of ways to make it perfectly clear that the story you are telling was composed by you to illustrate a point. While Jesus' parables may have been based on actual events, there is no reason to suppose that they were exact accounts of those events. They are, rather, stories depicting the sort of thing that everyone understands *might* be likely to happen at some time or other. They are customized, made precisely to order.

"But how does one go about that sort of thing? I have a hard enough time telling a story someone else has first told, let alone making up my own."

Probably you find it harder to repeat someone else's story, simply because it isn't your own. Don't you find it easier to tell about something you actually saw and heard—a firsthand experience?

"Well, yes, but . . ."

You see, when *you* make up your own stories, you may base them on real events that happened to you, or of which you were an observer, adapting them, as necessary, to fit the point you want to make. They are yours from the outset; you don't have to make them yours. And frequently stories that are composites of events in your life or the lives of your family or friends, or counseling cases from your own experiences, or events from your own general observation will work for you. Keep away from stories that others tell you or that you read in books. These are useful only when they trigger thought about some happening in which you participated in one way or another.

CREATING AN EXAMPLE

To help you understand what I am talking about, let's create an adapted example—right now, on the spot. I am doing this for the first time, as I write, with no forethought. Let's see now, . . . what truth from what passage should we illustrate? It will have to be one for which I have not previously developed any examples. I'm opening my New Testament at random (as you should never do when seeking guidance, of course). Hmmmm, 1 Timothy 5. My eye falls on verse 19: "Don't receive a charge against an elder unless it is supported by two or three witnesses." Okay, I have no examples for the verse. Good. Now, let's see, what do I know about that verse? Well, there is nothing special about the requirement to have two or three witnesses; that is standard practice with all Christians, not merely for elders (cf. Matt. 18:16; 2 Cor. 13:1, as well as Old Testament references). So, then, why does he make a point of it here when referring to elders? Because the elder, who has high visibility in a congregation, must at times make unpopular decisions, must rebuke various members of his church, and must do other tasks for which his motives may be misunderstood is a prime target for unfair criticism. And, he is vulnerable. Paul wants to preserve him so that vengeful people may not be able to overthrow his rule in the church. That is why he underscores this important biblical provision about testimony against an elder in this place.

Now, how can we make that point felt? How can we make it memorable (clarity isn't needed) for our listeners, so that they will be cautious not only about making charges but also about receiving them from others? An example would best do that, perhaps. But an example of *what?*

I've got it! I'll use an example that will make my listener think twice about making or receiving irresponsible charges against an elder by placing him in the position of one against whom unjust charges are made. Hmmmm, what story comes to mind? None, in particular. But wait, I can make up one out of a composite of instances I know or have heard about, adapting them to fit the point in this preaching portion.

There are cases of child abuse where, in some states, all it takes for the state to reach into your home and remove your children is the word of one spiteful neighbor. And you must engage a lawyer to get them back! I know of several such occurrences. So I can develop the particulars about frightened children, baffled and hysterical parents, and so on, from these. Then, having sketched the story in such a way that each member can enter into the horror and outrage of it, I can put it to them:

> Think how unfair it is. Think what it would be like for that to happen to you! All because you erected a fence to keep your neighbor's dog from running loose and trampling down your flowers. He swore he'd get you; but you never dreamed of anything so serious as this! He now claims that you are a child abuser because he heard your boy screaming after receiving a well-deserved spanking. Even though you will get your

child back through legal means, think of the harm this false accusation has done. His charge has brought about extreme suffering, caused unnecessary expense, and cast a shadow over you in the eyes of all who know about it.

Must I continue? Totally unshaped, unrefined, just as it rolled off the top of my head, you have followed me through the creation of an illustration that I will probably use someday. When charges that are not substantiated by witnesses are received, they can do untold harm. Many who could not understand the harm their loose tongues could cause by speaking against an elder can understand when they picture themselves in the position of an unjustly charged parent.

Of course, before using the above sketch, I'd shape it up, turning it into a real story with dialogue, recreating the tension of the drama. Then I'd draw the parallels between the falsely accused elder and the parent and point out the harm done in each case. I'd emphasize, especially, the personal injury done, the loss of authority that might result, the suspicion that is raised, and the assault on relationships within the church that may lead to ruptures.

Examples, properly developed and used, then, are an important part of effective applicatory preaching. Work on them. Perfect your skill at using them. The time and the effort will be well rewarded.

9

Applicatory Language

What is applicatory language? It is language that clearly indicates to the members of your congregation that you are talking to them about some aspect of their relationship to God or their neighbors. Language is applicatory when the combination of words, phrases, and sentences you use in preaching enables you to bring God's truth into forceful contact with the hearts of your listeners. It is the language of the successful herald.

There are those who tack on an application or two at the end of the sermon. Others apply as they go, drawing applications from each point. But, because they believe the whole sermon must apply to its hearers, effective preachers apply *as they speak*. The very language they use makes it apparent that they are speaking to the congregation about God and themselves *throughout* the sermon.

Applicatory language can be easily identified by the complex of characteristics that comprise it. It is dominated by the second person rather than the third, it is contemporary rather than obsolete, it is everyday speech rather than some literary form of speech, it is vivid rather than bland, it is concrete rather than abstract, it explodes with active verbs rather than moving sluggishly with passive verbs, it is simple rather than technical, it is straightforward—free from jargon, unnecessary complexity, and gaudy embellishment.

When people hear preaching with these winsome qualities, they listen to what the preacher has to say. Instinctively, they know that he has a message for them. On the contrary, language that is third-person dominated, obsolete, bland, abstract, passive, technical, full of jargon, and gaudy turns people off. They anticipate little from preaching like that, and that is usually what they get.

Probably the finest extended example of applicatory language in print is the Sermon on the Mount. Study it for its striking applicatory style and the refreshing absence of the tired clichés of nonapplicatory language. The shortest, most effective applicatory preaching on record is Jonah's clear, direct message, "Yet forty days and Nineveh shall be overthrown!"

Let me quote some sleep-inducing, heart-chilling, listener-repelling material:

> It appears to me at this climactic point in history that I am faced with a choice between my cherished freedoms and my mortal existence; I would prefer to lose the latter rather than the former.[1]

That sort of pompous, wordy speech is sure to deaden the liveliest Word from God. What Patrick Henry actually said, of course, was "Give me liberty or give me death!" The comparison shows the difference between applicatory and nonapplicatory language.

At the conclusion of Luther's second great speech before the Diet at Worms, he said:

> "Here I stand; I cannot do otherwise; so help me God! Amen."

Turn the average preacher loose on an occasion like that, and he might come up with something like this:

---

[1] Gene Olson, *Sweet Agony II* (Medford, Oreg.: Windyridge, 1983), 163.

"I have resolved to remain firm. I deem it impossible to retreat from the position I have taken heretofore. May the Most High God, who rules over the hearts and lives of men, grant me that grace and mercy of which I am in such dire need at the present moment. Amen and Amen."

Need I say more?

IT MEANS WORK

How can you avoid nonapplicatory language and learn to replace it with applicatory language? The same way all the great preachers of the past did—work at it!

Take Luther, for instance. When he first preached in a convent chapel to nuns, his sermons were full of the churchy, academic jargon in which his listeners were versed. But when he became pastor of the town church at Wittenberg, he realized that he "must make himself understood," he said, "by raw Saxons." How did he go about it?

Luther set to work doing several things. First, he worked hard on laundering his preaching to wash out starchy academic and technical terms. Obviously, he must have determined first what terminology was intelligible to his congregation and what was not. Second, he collected German proverbs and country sayings, listened to the popular language, and learned how to speak like those around him. Third, he used children for his standard of intelligibility: "I preach to little Hans and Elisabeth." If they could understand, others could too. Finally, he refused to play up to the educated in his congregation by the use of erudite language. He once said:

> "When I preach here at Wittenberg, I descend to the lowest level. I do not look at the doctors or masters, of whom about forty are present, but at the hundred or thousand young people. To them I preach. . . . If the others do not want to listen—the door is open."[2]

---

[2]In Ewald M. Plais, ed., *What Luther Says*, 3 vols. (St. Louis: Concordia, 1959), 3:1118–19. See also 1130.

In time, it was said of Luther, "It is impossible to misunderstand him."

Augustine, another highly educated intellectual, did much the same thing at Hippo in North Africa. He also preached to a mixed congregation. Although he had been a teacher of rhetoric, could speak eloquently, and was well-acquainted with all the tricks of the vocation, he chose to preach in the common rather than the literary Latin of his day. He declared that it was better to have the schoolmasters laughing than to have the people misunderstand. Accordingly, he aimed his words at the "poor artisans and fishermen" in his congregation.

CLARITY

Great preachers always aim at clarity. Indeed, clarity is not merely a desirable quality in a preacher, it is (as Paul said) an *obligation:*

> . . . so that I may proclaim it (the mystery) clearly *as I ought to.* (Col. 4:4)

It is not enough, then, to have a solid grasp on the meaning and purpose of a preaching portion, if, when you attempt to apply the message, you garble it by the language you use. One of the great language spoofs of all time is the sign that pointedly reads Eschew Obfuscation. It is a perfect example of what it forbids, with two obscure terms—one obsolescent, the other obtuse. Every preacher should post it in his study.

I open at random a book of sermons near at hand. I read,

> It were, however, a deprecation of the Cross to limit it to a remedy for sin: it is also, in Jesus' mind, a discipline of perfection for the soul.

Now, that language is intelligible, but stiff and formal; it is therefore not very forceful. It doesn't "grab" you. Let's see if we can do anything to improve it. How does this sound?

Don't limit the Cross. Jesus died for your sins on the Cross; but by it He also intends to change your whole life.

Do you see the difference? The first limps. Hindered by dull complexity and pompous structure, it stumbles over its own feet. The second strides forward, compelling you to listen. Perhaps if I were to spend more time (I took about three minutes improving the sentence), I could do far better. But, as you can see, even a few simple alterations have changed nonapplicatory into applicatory language. Notice, I have made two sentences out of one. That simplifies. I have personalized it, directing it to the listener as a message from God to him. I have removed dull, abstract nouns like *deprecation, discipline,* and *perfection,* rewording the sentence so that verbs speak concretely to the listener about himself. And I have substituted for its wooden bookishness a contraction of the sort you hear in everyday speech: "Don't."

You must learn to preach so that each listener knows you are talking to him or her. That will happen only when you use language as personal as a toothbrush. Lectures are delivered to masses; sermons are preached to individuals.

Here is a sentence from a sermon for you to practice on. Using the ideas presented thus far in this chapter, personalize it: modify words and phrases to make it applicatory. Rewrite the entire sentence if you wish. Write your improved version in the space below it:

It is reasonable to expect that Jesus' idea of salvation will correspond with His idea of sin, as lock and key, or disease and medicine, and one is not disappointed.

USE UP-TO-DATE LANGUAGE

Obsolete word uses and constructions, like obsolete words, tend to repel. Truth does not grow old and obsolete, but language does. Reading through H. L. Mencken's first *Supplement to the American Language,* I was struck by the number of words that have either changed meaning or dropped out of usage since that book was written some fifty years ago. It does not take long for words to become worn or even die. When we use such terms, what we say takes on the same character as the word itself.

People may not know why the language of their preacher sounds wrong, but they do recognize obsolescence when they hear it. It is like wearing wide ties when narrow ones are "in." When people say, "He *sounds* like a preacher," they are not always referring to content. What they may have in mind is his dated language (or his ministerial tone). The ministry has preserved much that has long since disappeared from ordinary, everyday language. Preachers should stay current linguistically. There is no excuse for using stained-glass language that turns the young people off and makes their parents wonder. The use of dated words and phrases is particularly offensive when they are spoken in funereal tones. The New Testament was written in the current, common (*koinē*) language of the apostles. Preach in the newscaster language of the day. That is the modern "koine." Here are a few commonly heard constructions and uses that you should avoid:

1. The use of "for" for "because," or "since" ("We'll not need it, Tom, for he's found one already"). Sometimes, in constructions like these, it is better not to replace "for" at all. Simply omit it, using a semicolon's worth of pause instead: "Forgive me, Lord; (for) I have sinned."

2. The use of archaic possessive constructions: "the Word of God," "the pride of man." Say, instead, "God's Word" and "human pride."

3. The use of outdated words: for "sepulcher," say *tomb*; for "unto," say *to*; for "yea," say *yes!* or *certainly* or *surely*; for "lest," say *so that you won't.*

4. And, as we have seen in the improved sentence above, use contractions whenever it's possible to do so (there's, didn't, don't, won't, etc.). For "Let us pray," say "Let's pray." There are no rules for the use of contractions. A speaker must learn to sense when they are fitting and when they are not. This comes only from listening carefully to actual speech. Printed material uses fewer contractions than oral English.

5. To express a prayer or wish, use the correct term "may" rather than "might." Say "May (not might) there be many days like these!" And pray, "May (not might) Mary be healed. . . ."

Many other preacher foibles could be mentioned, but, basically, what is needed is to become aware of the problem and begin listening for nonapplicatory language in your preaching. Studying tape recordings of your sermons should help. When you detect something wrong, learn how to say it better and practice the new way until it takes the place of the old.

While you're at it, stop making up words like "needful" (use *necessary* instead) or "prideful" (say *proud*).

"How about slang? Should I use it?"

Yes, but use it sparingly, correctly, when up to date and appropriate. Use it when it best says what you want to say, when it sets your words in the context of a particular tone you wish to effect, and when, because it is appropriate to the subject matter, it doesn't offend good (I didn't say pedantic) taste.

I have mentioned the fact that active rather than passive verbs help make language applicatory. Compare these two sentences:

It is thought that you might have become ill.

People think you're sick.

The first sounds like something Jeeves the Butler might have said to Bertie Wooster in one of P. G. Wodehouse's novels. The second, without calling attention to itself, says what you want to say in good old colloquial English.

The simplicity of sentences with active verbs is what gives them force. Passive verbal constructions—proper in their place—lose power because of their relative complexity. They hesitate. Use them, therefore, when you want to come in at the back door. Active verbs walk right up on the porch and knock on the front door.

Also avoid constructions using the verb "to be" plus an adjective. For example, in the last paragraph I wrote, "They hesitate." Instead, I might have written (less forcefully), "They are hesitant." You can sense the difference in the two constructions as you read back over them.

And not enough can be said for concreteness. Don't say "thing" if you can specifically name it. Don't say "car"; say "Chevy." Use colorful illustrations that your audience recognizes: for "traitor," say "Judas." Concreteness appeals to the imagination; it enables people to picture what you are talking about. Go back over some sermon tapes, find places where concrete nouns and verbs might be substituted for abstract ones, and notice the difference it makes.

"But how can I learn to do these things? I can't think about them while I'm preaching."

No, of course you can't—and shouldn't. But if you set aside some time each day to work on them, eventually you will find that what you have practiced outside the pulpit will overflow into the pulpit.

Set aside a period of time, perhaps the time it takes you to drive home for supper each day, to rehearse some brief event that you plan to tell during the supper hour. Work on the best way to phrase sentences, the best words to use. Think about how you can replace weak, habitual constructions with strong, fresh ones. Then, as you tell your story, consciously take the time to say it well.

While you dare not think about such things while preaching (you must focus on content, God, and your congregation), there is one thing you can do beforehand. In preparing the full-sentence outline that you take into the pulpit, concentrate on the language you choose. Spell out key constructions to guide you as you speak from the outline.

Language is important. We who believe in the verbal inspiration and inerrancy of the Bible, of all people, ought to be aware of this. By language you convey the sense of authority, urgency, importance, warning, or hope that inheres in God's written message. On the other hand, poor language may undercut any or all of these nuances. Language that is not pertinent is impertinent.

Good language is at once clear, simple, direct, personal, active, and concrete. Work hard on filling your mouth with such language. You must not fail to apply God's truth to your congregation simply because you lack the vocabulary and skill with words to do the job. Language is the preacher's stock in trade. Any preacher who does not continue to work on language usage throughout his ministry isn't worthy of the position. The Bible is as pertinent and up-to-date as tomorrow's newspaper; the language in which you proclaim its truth must match it.

10

Applicatory Conclusions

Obviously, from what I have been saying so far, you
know I am not going to suggest that you save the application for the end. This approach, developed in the Middle
Ages and mediated into English Protestantism by the Puritans, has passed down to our time in various forms. Sometimes in the Puritans' sermons there is a whole section
devoted to application (remember the Puritan "uses"?);[1] but
more likely today, application is reserved till the last point or
the conclusion. Typical of the sort of sermon in which the

---

[1]Of Baxter's preaching it was said, "He began with a careful unfolding of
the text, proceeded to the removal of possible difficulties or objections,
made an application of the uses of the text, and came at last to a fervent
appeal" (emphasis mine): quoted by Harry C. Howard, *Princess of the
Christian Pulpit and Pastorate*, second series (Nashville: Cokesbury, 1928),
90.

While a "fervent appeal" is highly appropriate for a conclusion, one
wonders whether today, when there are so many other things to do and
think about, a congregation will wait for a preacher to plod through all the
content mentioned here before making that appeal. Applicatory sermons
appeal from the outset. Chalmers, in contrast to Baxter, developed an idea
"continually recurring throughout . . . in argument, illustration and application" (Ibid., 158). This method sounds closer to the applicatory sermon.

final main point is devoted to application is one by W. T. Holland. The outline shows how it is done:

I. What does this text mean?
II. Why is this text so necessary to a church?
III. How can we apply this text to our lives?[2]

In other cases, the application is reserved for the last subpoint under one or more main points, fracturing the unity of the sermon and demanding a highly repetitious summary and interrelationship between the various applications in the conclusion. Or the whole may be left as it is, in its essential treelike form, applications hanging like persimmons from every branch. So-called Bible teachers, homiletical magicians, and many "expository" preachers opt for this last approach.

Alexander, rightly concerned about this sort of thing, wrote:

"Applications" mar the unity of a discourse. . . . When three or four heads of application are appended (that is 'tacked on'), the mind is first drawn one way and then another, and frequently altogether away from the body of the discourse. Every sermon tends *in some direction*: let it take that direction; it is the proper ending. The superstitious reverence for an application of several points, cuts up this part of the sermon (the conclusion), short enough at best, and does not allow time to rise upon the wing, or to kindle a flame.[3]

Henry Ward Beecher's last sermon, preached on February 27, 1887, was reprinted in the *Brooklyn Eagle* of June 1910. The sermon was on Luke 16:4. A reproduction of the written outline from which he preached was included. It has four main heads. Then follows, in the place of a conclusion, the word *Apply*, under which are five numbered applications, jotted down as catch phrases:

---

[2]W. T. Holland, "The Peace of the Church," in *The Zondervan 1983 Pastor's Annual* (Grand Rapids: Zondervan, 1982), 302–4.

[3]James W. Alexander, *Thoughts on Preaching* (Edinburgh: Banner of Truth Trust, 1975), 22.

1. Christian life only understood (undecipherable word
   here) as Duty—as Happy

2. Only Honorable one—

3. Enter to right—

4. Beware of weakening the Purpose—

5. Lay aside all ideas of later Repentance—

That is what Alexander was talking about: fracturing
the unity of the sermon, scattering one's shot. Beecher had a
tremendous influence on the homileticians who taught the
last generation of preachers (and homileticians!). That is
one reason why we find this practice continuing today.

The preaching of Robert G. Lee is typical. Speaking of
the "concluding few moments" of the sermon, his biogra-
pher says, "An invitation is then given, or the message is
applied personally to those in the audience."[4] Note well, to
the conclusion was allotted the "concluding few moments."
According to Schuyler English, into the earlier part of the
sermon Lee "deposits all of this study, preparation, discrimi-
nation, lore, and experience," accompanied by "his vast
vocabulary," while his listeners sit "in awe and admiration
of the orator."[5]

I have been trying to persuade you that all of these
approaches are inadequate, often self-defeating. The application should not be "saved" for the end or some place near
the end. It should begin with the first sentence and continue
throughout. It should capture and hold the listener with its
personal relevance at every point—including the conclusion. Throughout the sermon, everything you say about
problems as well as solutions, about the meaning of the
preaching portion as well as how people think and live
today, should be said in such a way that the congregation
knows you are talking about them in relationship to God
and their neighbors. And, as we will see, when the whole
sermon is applicatory, it is not necessary to sum up in some

---

[4]E. Schuyler English, *Robert G. Lee: A Chosen Vessel* (Grand Rapids:
Zondervan, 1949), 268.

[5]Ibid., 268, 317.

grand application at the end. The space can be used for some additional purpose.

THE INDUCTIVE APPLICATORY SERMON

Yet, having said all that, I want also to assert that it is possible—and at times necessary—to save solutions and answers for the end of the message. This more inductive approach may best be reserved (as Stephen was well aware; Acts 7) for those times when you are addressing a hostile crowd. True, he was stoned but not before he had his say. Had he preached deductively, chances are he would have been stoned long before he had delivered even a small portion of his message. So there are exceptions to what I have been emphasizing so strongly.

Throughout the message inductive preaching gathers particulars together that lead to a general conclusion. It is a form of argumentation. Deductive preaching, on the other hand, states the conclusion and then spells out the particulars that led to it. Most week-by-week preaching in a congregation that respects God's Word and is anxious to hear it proclaimed ought to be deductive. The deductive preacher has the opportunity to emphasize God's message to His people over and over again from various angles. Since they hear it throughout, he does not need to waste time in the conclusion summing up, or making the point of the sermon for the first time, but can devote that important space to other things. It is easier to make the entire sermon applicatory when preaching deductively—the application of the *telos* is continually held before the listener.

How may one preach inductively and yet be sure the entire sermon is applicatory? It is harder, but it can be done. The fundamental goal is to keep the congregation involved in what you are saying throughout the sermon. To do this, you must make them understand that the particulars they are learning are relevant to some problem you posed in the introduction, a problem whose solution they are eager to hear. In various ways, you must keep on telling them (often subtly, when possible) that what you are saying will inevitably lead to that solution. You may ask them question after question from time to time to hold interest and build suspense. But—and this is the big "but" about the inductive sermon—the climactic solution *must not disappoint.* When you have built up expectations throughout the better part of a half hour or more and then in the conclusion throw out some commonplace answer to the questions you have been posing, your sermon will fizzle. It will disappoint, anger, frustrate, and confuse. You probably won't get the same listeners to follow you on another such trip.

Everything in the inductive applicatory sermon points toward the conclusion. The conclusion is therefore all-important. The effectiveness of the entire sermon depends on it. You may fail elsewhere, but you must not fail here. The conclusion must not be a letdown. It must fulfill its promise by satisfying the listener's desire to know. The whole sermon has elements like those in a good introduction, elements that create a desire to hear more and more—and more. An Acts 2:12 attitude ("What does this mean?") is fostered from beginning to end. What I said about creating an event, therefore, pertains also to the inductive applicatory sermon as a whole. In a very real sense, this sort of sermon, when properly constructed, is itself a strung-out, tension-sustaining event. Because of these facts, you can see that fulfillment at the end is critical.

The inductive applicatory sermon cannot be preached frequently. It is too intense. It creates too many expectations, and therefore it is too likely to fail. The sermon is a species of high drama. That does not appertain to every message you will preach; many passages neither demand nor allow it. It should be reserved, therefore, for hostile audiences, where you want to make your point before they shout you down, and for those special occasions that require drastic, dramatic change.

In all cases, it should be apparent from what I have said that the applicatory conclusion is not "tacked on," even in the inductive sermon—when it is well-constructed. Indeed, it is the inevitable outcome of that sermon; it is the climax, the high point at which all tension finds resolution.

THE DEDUCTIVE APPLICATORY SERMON

The conclusion to deductive applicatory sermons may also be climactic. The danger here, however, is the possibility of its becoming anticlimactic. Having said so much about the *telos* of the preaching portion from various perspectives, a conclusion *may* become merely a restatement. That can be dull and anticlimactic, closing an otherwise effective sermon on a sour note. Avoid redundancy at all costs!

"How can I do that?"

There are several possibilities. The conclusion may consist of an encouraging or motivational story relating to what has been said. The story of the two foundations at the conclusion of the Sermon on the Mount is of this sort. Jesus recapitulates nothing, sums up nothing. What He does instead is say, "Turn these teachings into life or you will be swept away by life's storms." Probably you will want to conclude many sermons with an encouraging or motivational story. It is especially appropriate when you have made the *telos* of the preaching portion explicit from the outset and repetition in the conclusion would add little. Let's take a look at a motivational conclusion.

In a sermon on Philippians 3:20–4:1, in which I am talking about the listener's citizenship in heaven, I end with Edward Everett Hale's story *The Man Without a Country.*

I sketch the story: A criminal cursed his country; he said he never wanted to see it again. The judge sentenced him to realize his wish. For the rest of his life he sailed the ocean, never being allowed to go ashore. No one was ever allowed to say a word to him about his homeland. All news of it was cut out of newspapers.

Then I bring home to those who are not citizens of the heavenly country the need to trust Christ, in order to acquire citizenship in the wonderful country about which they have been hearing throughout the sermon. I say something like this: If you are not a citizen of heaven, you will be banished too. You may turn your back on Jesus Christ, but you will be judged for it. You will be forbidden forever to step on the heavenly shores. You have no lasting citizenship here on earth, and none to look forward to there. You will sail the seas of hell *forever.* There will be no contact with heaven and those who live in it. Hell is filled with men and women without a country! They are "wandering stars, for whom the blackness of darkness is reserved forever."

TYPES OF CONCLUSIONS

There are many other ways to end an applicatory sermon. You may wish to end with a series of questions that put the point of the sermon to the listener. Consider this conclusion:

> Is not life desirable? Can a soul be in love with death? Or is death so inevitable that it is vain for you to flee from it? Or is there some barrier in your way? Or is God not really willing to remove the death and bestow the life? Are these the reasons? Or what answer do you mean to make to God's question, so urgently, so importunately put and pressed home on you, "Why will you die?"[6]

What a powerful conclusion! Seven sentences, each ending in a pointed question—to make the listener think.

In another sermon, a series of questions may not be as appropriate as a series of exhortations. Questions make one think; exhortations are more to the purpose when there is nothing more to think about; when mere obedience is what is required. Maltbie D. Babcock closes a sermon with this paragraph chock-full of directives:

> Keep your feet on the solid ground of reality, and do something tangible. *Do* His will; don't *suffer* it. You are the light of the world;—then shine! Light that is covered is not light, for men still walk in darkness. You are the salt of the earth. If it be covered up, it not only loses its savor, but, worse yet, destroys its reason for being, since it is a preservative. Put yourself at the decaying points of social life and stop the putrefaction. Because past generations have not done all that they might, that is

---

[6]Horatius Bonar, *Fifty-two Sermons* (Grand Rapids: Baker, 1954), 329.

only an additional reason why we should do all we possibly can."[7]

From the same book comes a conclusion that embodies an example:

Our Lord commissions us to do something for Him. You are members of the body of Christ. I want to pick up that book. The head flashes the command to the hand, but the hand does not move. What does this mean? I see a physician, and he says, "Incipient paralysis," and all that can possibly be done is done to effect a cure. But how about us? When the Spirit of Jesus Christ lays His commands on us, do we always respond? If we do not, the members are not obeying the dictate of the Head, and to the degree that we fail our spiritual life is paralyzed.[8]

Babcock's conclusion also exhibits another trait that many preachers have found effective—ending the last sentence on an unresolved note of tension. The tension so presented can be resolved only by the proper response of the listener. Calvin sometimes did this. So did Luther. Let us note a conclusion to one of Luther's sermons. Not only is there tension but intertwined is a warning and a threat!

And if you will not love one another, God will send a great plague upon you; let this be a warning to you, for God will not reveal His Word and have it preached in vain. You are tempting God too far, my friends. If some one in times past had preached the Word to our forefathers, they would perchance have acted differently. Or if the Word were preached today to many poor children in the cloisters, they would receive it with much greater joy than you. You do not heed it at all, and give yourselves to other things, which are unnecessary and foolish. I commend you to God.[9]

---

[7]Maltbie D. Babcock, *Fragments That Remain* (New York: Revell, 1907), 187.

[8]Ibid., 201.

[9]Martin Luther, *Works of Martin Luther* (Philadelphia: Holman, 1915), 2:421.

As you can see, not only does Luther leave the situation with God and the congregation, in doing so (incidentally), notice how he tells it like it is. There is not only tension and warning and threat, there is also bold preaching. No wonder God used Luther, with all his faults, to bring about a reformation—he was fearless in proclaiming God's truth!

But there are still other ways in which to end a deductive sermon. At the conclusion of my sermon on Lot, I end with a strong appeal. I have been talking about compromise and its effects throughout the sermon. Then I conclude, in words something like these (I preach extempore):

> Do you really think that the Sodom toward which you are about to pitch your tent is so different? Do you really think that you are so much stronger than Lot? "It won't happen to me," you say. That's what they all say! Consider carefully what you are doing—to yourself, to your wife, to your children.
>
> But perhaps you are already living in Sodom; you are even an elder of the city. Repent! Get out before it's too late! "But my connections, my business, my roots ...!" Yes, yes, I know all that. But God's angels are coming. Get out while you can save your family, your future, your faith. Reestablish your testimony for the Lord. Get out! Get out! ... I beg you: get out!

James Moffatt has a conclusion in which the appeal is somewhat different. You can feel the pathos in the two pleading questions embedded in it. They are actually indicative sentences in which he raises the pitch only at the end:

> Some of us may be just where Joab was, with a good record behind us and the last treacherous temptations of middle age rising beside us. Let us say to ourselves and to one another, "You won't give way at the close? You won't spoil your record by dropping the old flag at this time of day?" For what is faithfulness to God if it is not faithfulness to death, a faithfulness that will not

betray Him or desert Him in the afternoon or in the evening any more than in the morning hours?[10]

Sometimes an explanation is in order. A. T. Pierson ends a sermon with an explanation of repentance, using an example rather than the abstract term itself:

> Tell me how long it would take to change from death to life. Just as long, and no longer, as it takes you to turn around. Your back has been on God. You turn, and your face is toward him. It will take no longer for a sinner to become a living son of God than that. Just put your heart into your acceptance of Jesus. Cast your whole will into the Fatherhood of God, renounce your sin and your rebellion, and take the salvation that is given to you as freely as the sun gives its light, or the spring gives its stream; and before you turn round to go out that church door, you may have this salvation, and perhaps enjoy in yourself the consciousness that you are saved![11]

Sometimes there is a dramatic build-up that reaches its climax in the conclusion. This is what Alexander was talking about when he spoke of rising on wings in the conclusion. Here is a fine example of one such conclusion. It is from an older French preacher but still has impact today—especially when read at the close of the entire sermon:

> No, this will not do, my dear brother! We must *personally* love. O moments lost forever, in which, during the whole course of your life, you might have loved God, might have learned to love Him, might have accustomed yourself to love Him! Precious moments! in which Divine grace solicited your heart—in which all the obstinacy of your malice it was necessary to resist! Then, then, God spoke! His mind and His heart are shut against your misery! Your mind and your heart are shut against His mercy! What do you expect but the rigors of His justice? My hearers, you still possess these precious moments! God addresses you while I address you!

---

[10]James Moffatt, *Reasons and Reasons* (London: Hodder and Stoughton, 1911), 101.

[11]Arthur T. Pierson, *The Gospel* (Grand Rapids: Baker, 1978), 39.

Expect not that these moments will never pass away! Make use of them in the exercise of a prompt repentance! So be it—in the name of the Father, of the Son, and of the Holy Spirit![12]

Count the lines in the above quotation and then count the exclamation points! That is emotional preaching—rhetoric rising on the wings of emotion in pleading with the lost. How well does your earnest concern for the lost burst forth in unrestrained passion? Or is it bottled up within because you failed to think through and plan your conclusions?

As one last way to close a message, let me suggest that implementation is always appropriate, but it is especially so when people have tried and failed many times. It is often true that the missing note in evangelical preaching is the "how to" emphasis. The Sermon on the Mount is filled with how-to implementation. From a long conclusion to one of Babcock's sermons, I will extract a few lines of implementation:

If your life seems gloomy and hard and sordid and without sources of thankfulness, try this plan:—do one kind act every day. A friend once said to me . . . "For years I have made it a rule to do at least one kind act every day, and one night, no longer ago than last week, I got into bed, and suddenly remembered that I had done no consciously kind act that day; so I got up, made a light, wrote a letter to a woman in trouble, and enclosed a check."[13]

When you save implementation for the conclusion, you may want to combine it with dialogue:

---

[12]Charles De La Rue, in Henry C. Fish, *Pulpit Eloquence* (New York: M. W. Wood, 1857), 2:94–95.

[13]Babcock, *Fragments*, 74. As W. B. Selbie says, "The preacher can never allow his audience to escape the question: what are you going to do about it?" (*This Ministry* (London: Student Movement Press, 1932), 36). One way to squelch any excuses is to provide clear, concrete examples of how it might be done. Peter did this in answer to that very question (Acts 2:37–38). See also the directions John the Baptist gave (Luke 3:10–14).

"What you say is all very fine, preacher, but *how* do I go about it? Where do I begin?"

"Good question! In closing I want to give you one or two suggestions about how to get started. First. . . ."

Now, since this is a conclusion, you must be sure that these implementations are brief (if you must develop them in full, don't wait until the conclusion; use the last point in the message to do so). Sometimes the very best conclusion is a combination of how-to implementation demonstrated by an example, as in Babcock's conclusion above. It always takes the edge off an objection to see how others have succeeded in kneading God's truth into the dough of daily living. Stories help sustain interest to the very end and give encouragement as well as provide needed direction.

THE PERSONAL NOTE

Occurring in all of these conclusions is one feature that you should not miss: the personal note. In it, the preacher uses the second-person pronoun freely. He gets down to cases and says some very pointed things. Go back over the quotations in this chapter and examine them with this in mind.

Then take a look at these words, as the preacher draws near to his conclusion:

I know that I am probing some hearts here today to their inner recesses. You are busy and occupied and useful, but you are not satisfied. "Yes," you say, "I am!" Honestly? Is there no hunger? no restlessness? no longing to know the truth of the stronger God who has demolished your dreams? . . . You hear the ticking of the clock that marks the passing of time, and you know that it is slipping away from you. You hear the pulses of that faithful little organ, the heart—beat, beat, beat!— steady throbbing of your life. And you think how that life is passing on—how ideals are not being realized, how purposes are not being attained—and you wonder if it is worthwhile to live. You recognize the dismemberment of your idol, and the dismemberment of an idol is hard to face. You know your life is bringing you no satisfaction. And the steady beat, beat, beat goes on, irresistible. What will you do?[14]

There is one situation in which a summary of the main points is useful and highly appropriate. That is when the sermon was built around steps necessary to attain a certain goal. And if each step is essential, so that omitting even one would lead to failure, a summary stressing that fact may be the most fitting conclusion.

Summaries are also useful when following the steps of a process in a definite order is important. For example, "Remember," you may want to say, "you cannot expect God to accept your worship until you first are reconciled to your neighbor."

One final word: a conclusion must conclude. A conclusion must be prepared very carefully beforehand; it is too important to leave to the inspiration of the moment. Preachers who have not carefully thought through their conclusions tend to fall into one of two traps:

1. They fizzle out at the end, rather than ending strongly. They often rely on stock clichés like "And may God bless this message to each and every one of you" or, in lieu of anything better, "Amen!"

2. They drag the message on beyond its natural concluding point, adding material when everyone sensed it was time to stop. Sometimes this results in two or even three "conclusions," none of which is actually a conclusion at all.

End strongly. In introducing Chuck Swindoll at a Congress on Exposition, Ray Stedman said, "Chuck really needs no introduction; but he could use a conclusion!" Never let what was said there in jest be said in all seriousness of you.

---

[14]Babcock, *Fragments,* 139–41.

11

Applicatory Knowledge

To apply God's truth throughout a message, it is absolutely necessary for the preacher to understand the culture of his day, issues abroad in society, community affairs, and the ethos of his own particular congregation. Otherwise he may *think* he is applying the truth when all he is doing is missing the mark. The applicatory preacher, therefore, carefully studies the preaching milieu.

To apply truth properly, you must understand people: their personal problems, the pressures their acquaintances exert on them, the propaganda with which the media daily bombards them, and the intracongregational dynamics that influence them for good or ill. That is to say, to be an applicatory preacher, you must become thoroughly conversant with your culture.

Of course, the Bible teaches many edifying truths that you may readily preach to any congregation, in any culture, at any time. That is one reason why application from a book thousands of years old is possible. Truth is timeless; principles that were valid then still apply. At bottom, human beings and human problems do not change, but their expression, color, and shape do. And there are many other preaching portions in which the application of God's truth to any given congregation is not immediately apparent.

MR. FACING-TWO-WAYS

We have seen that application involves two entities brought together in forceful contact: God's truth and the members of your church. Neither may be considered abstractly. Initially, God applied His truth to a person, or persons, living at a particular time and place in history. But He also gave His revelation to His church in every age. In bridging the gap, the preacher's knowledge of his people and his times is vital.

The following diagram illustrates the situation:

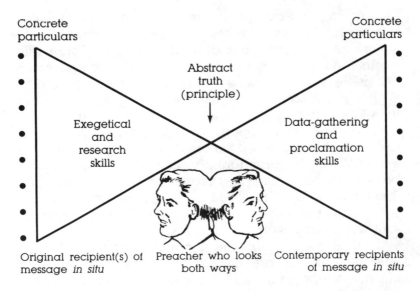

Concrete particulars

Concrete particulars

Abstract truth (principle)

Exegetical and research skills

Data-gathering and proclamation skills

Original recipient(s) of message *in situ*   Preacher who looks both ways   Contemporary recipients of message *in situ*

As you can see, the preacher's knowledge and understanding of persons, places, times, and circumstances must extend in two directions. He must learn all he can about the original recipient(s) of the message and the occasion that gave rise to the message in order to understand both

1. The truth, and
2. The sort of people and situation(s) to which it applies.

He must know as fully as possible the congregation (the contemporary recipients) to which he preaches to understand:

1. If the truth applies to any or all of them and, if so,
2. How it does.

SOME AND ALL

To begin with, notice in number 1 above the phrase "if the truth applies to any or all of them." It is important to distinguish between some and all (cf. 1 Cor. 11:18). In addressing congregations both our Lord and His apostles regularly did so. In the messages to the seven churches, found in the Book of Revelation, Jesus says some things to whole churches (cf. 3:14ff.) and some things to groups within them (2:10, 14–15, 24; 3:4, 9). And at the conclusion of each letter, he makes an individualized appeal:

"Whoever has an ear, let him hear what the Spirit says to the churches."

Doubtless, this meant not only to *heed* His words, but also to determine, individually, *which* of His words apply.

So it is possible to preach to a whole congregation. These letters indicate that congregations, as a whole, do take on a kind of personality (note the message to Laodicea in which no distinctions are made). But they also indicate (as do most of the epistles) that there may be groups and individuals within any given congregation to whom a particular message applies. These fundamental facts must be kept in mind not only when considering the selection of a preaching portion but also when making application of the truth within it.

Just as Jesus was aware that the original congregations were sometimes divided and sometimes compact, in making application of a truth today as you preach you must

1. Choose to speak to one group in one sermon and, at a later time, to another group in a second sermon, or

2. Preach from a passage that views one applicable truth from the two or more perspectives that prevail in the congregation.

The temptation will be to divide your sermon into two so as to address everyone. But unless the original passage warrants such an approach, you will end up weakening the thrust of your message. You cannot say everything in one sermon. Unless the groups are diametrically opposed to each other (so that anything said strikes both groups from opposite directions), it is better to speak of separate matters on separate occasions.

GATHER FACTS

In his introduction to *The Chicago Statement on Biblical Application*, J. I. Packer wrote:

> Application of biblical principles to life is always conditioned by the limits of our factual knowledge about the situation in which it is being made.[1]

Packer warns that unless a preacher's knowledge of the contemporary situation to which he applies his message is both accurate and complete, he may aim at the wrong target. How is a pastor to gather data that he needs so that he can preach with confidence?

First, he will rely on information given directly to him by his elders. Because he cannot be everywhere in the church at all times, he will rely on the elders, who are constantly out among the people. If elders are functioning as they should, each will have a smaller group of members assigned to

---

[1]J. I. Packer, *The Chicago Statement on Biblical Application*, Summit III (Walnut Creek, Calif.: International Council on Biblical Inerrancy, 1987), 11.

him, a group over whom he carefully exercises oversight. This superintendence, or oversight, should be regular and extensive. It should include home visits, small gatherings, counseling, and ministry of other sorts. Each elder should be so intimately acquainted with his portion of the congregation that he would be able, upon inquiry, to answer basic questions about them that the pastor might ask before preaching a particular sermon. Cooperation with elders can be all-important.[2]

Moreover, the pastor, through counseling, personal contact, and oversight as a ruling elder himself, should be among his people regularly, acquiring the data he needs to make accurate evaluations. He, along with the other ruling elders, will be good shepherds of the sheep only when they are able to call them by name and know their individual eccentricities. When you have gone through the deep waters, traveled through the valley of the shadow in which death lurks, healed many a wound, brought back the strays, then, and then only, do you get to know the peculiar foibles of your flock.

But the preacher will also be keenly aware of the local, national, and international influences that are brought to bear on the congregation. He will keep in touch with events in his community. He will be conscious of movements on the national and international scene. He will know the sorts of things that are being said on TV, in newspapers and news magazines, etc. In general, he will be a person who is as keenly aware of the milieu in which his people live and how it is likely to influence them as the Old Testament prophets were aware of the times and circumstances in which the people to whom they preached lived. He will be able to discern the "signs of the times."

When he hears rumors, he will ask for evidence from those who pass them on. He will trace gossip to its sources. He will make those who spread charges substantiate them

---

2See Howard Vanderwell, *Preaching That Connects* (Fullerton, Calif.: R. C. Law, 1989), for a comprehensive program involving one's elders in making preaching decisions.

by one or two witnesses (2 Cor. 13:1). When he has such witness, he will take his witnesses with him to face the person or persons they are charging with sin, or he will name the witnesses to the one being charged (1 Cor. 1:11). In other words, in his sermons he will not accuse his congregation of offenses that come by way of third parties (even the elders will responsibly inform him of specific matters on the basis of evidence and witnesses) who will not stand by their accusations. He will always deal with such matters on a private basis according to Matthew 18:15ff.[3] rather than making them the subject of messages.

However, when he uncovers a nest of problems involving large numbers of people, he may be forced to deal with them in a more public way. When he discovers the same problem occurring again and again among various persons and families, he will want to preach about it to help those in trouble and to warn others about the gaping sinkhole into which so many seem to be falling.

He will notice where the Jehovah's Witnesses, the Mormons, and other groups are currently going from door to door, and as he sees them approaching the areas in which his constituency live, he will anticipate them by a series of messages that will prepare his people for their coming. In general, if the preacher is one who buries himself in his study, among musty tomes, he will hardly be able to fulfill the task of a faithful preacher of the Word.

MAKE APPLICATORY CHOICES

"But I preach through books of the Bible. I simply let the Lord choose my texts. In that way, I cover everything, preach on subjects I wouldn't preach on otherwise, and let the chips fall where they may."

Naturally, there is nothing wrong with preaching through books of the Bible, but if you think that by doing so you will not need to know the specific needs and problems

---

[3]For details on how to handle such matters, see my *Handbook of Church Discipline* (Grand Rapids: Zondervan, 1986).

of your congregation, you are wrong. First, there are sixty-six books in the Bible. You make a decision about what to preach no less than does the preacher who chooses from a different text each week. The only difference is that your decision to preach on a particular book of the Bible is much more momentous than his. If you commit yourself to a course of exposition through a whole book, you may have made a colossal error by choosing a book that is not as pertinent to them at the moment as another might be. If it is your practice to preach through books, *all the more* do you need to know your congregation.

Also, preaching through a Bible book does not relieve you of the responsibility of knowing your congregation, since you must still apply each preaching portion you encounter. To apply truth accurately you must have such knowledge.

So, in conclusion, I urge you to take the time and make the effort (both of which must be considerable) to get to know not only the scriptural persons and places involved in a message but also those involved in the reception of that message today. All the other work you do will be in vain if you are aiming at shadows in the underbrush rather than real live animals.

12

Conclusion

Speaking of the preaching of Jesus, which was always so fresh, so natural, so applicatory, William Curtis says,

> We are tempted to think that His words cost Him nothing, that He was so wise that wisdom flowed as by necessity, from his mouth . . . that he underwent no struggle of preparation, no sweat of the brow before He attained the perfection of His message.[1]

Curtis rightly thinks that Jesus spent the long, silent hours of which the gospels give us hints but no details, prayerfully working out the content and form of what He would say. Curtis is undoubtedly correct in inferring this from the fact that Jesus was true man as well as true God. The Bible says that He "grew" in stature, but also in wisdom (Luke 2:52)— that is, in His knowledge of the truth and how to present it.

If this is so, there is every reason for you to work diligently at the same task. Thinking of preaching as the application of biblical truth to contemporary situations

[1]William A. Curtis, *Jesus Christ the Teacher* (London: Oxford University Press, 1944), 15.

according to the way God applied it should provide a helpful milieu in which to do so. It should go a long way toward converting your approach from a lecturing to a preaching stance. It should help you think of people—the people to whom you will be speaking—as you prepare your message. It should give you a new sense of the breadth of God's Word as you see the extent to which a given principle may be applied (Ps. 119:96).

When you stand before your people to preach, you will recognize that there is no need to "perform," to exhibit your knowledge of the past and your mastery of the Bible. You are entering the pulpit to bring God's message, fresh from the Scriptures to the people in your congregation. You are going to preach the passage you have chosen as Calvin did—as if your people were the first to hear it, as a message David, Jesus, or Paul is delivering specifically to your church. When that begins to happen—as it will when you begin to get the hang of applicatory preaching—you will recognize its effects by the way your people begin to talk about the Bible. They will speak of it as a Book that confronts them rather than as a mere history of God's dealings long ago. And you will recognize it when you begin to see the changes this will make in their daily living.

For them, God will become real. For you, preaching will become a joy. And in it all God will be honored, and the name of Jesus Christ will be exalted. That is what it is all about!

Subject Index

Name Index

Shepard, Jean, 100
Spurgeon, Charles H., 71
Stedman, Ray, 129
Stifler, J. M., 61
Vanderwell, Howard, 135

Vos, Gerhardus, 20
Wagner, Roger, 62
Whitefield, George, 71
Wodehouse, P. G., 113

Scripture Index

TRUTH APPLIED